What They Don't Teach You in Sales 101

What They Don't Teach You in Sales 101

Steven R. Drozdeck

Joseph Yeager

Linda Sommer

McGraw-Hill, Inc.

New York St. Louis San Francisco Auckland Bogotá
Caracas Hamburg Lisbon London Madrid
Mexico Milan Montreal New Delhi Paris
San Juan São Paulo Singapore
Sydney Tokyo Toronto

Library of Congress Cataloging-in-Publication Data

Drozdeck, Steven R.
   What they don't teach you in sales 101 / Steven Drozdeck, Joseph
Yeager, Linda Sommer.
      p.   cm.
   Includes index.
   ISBN 0-07-017865-8 : — ISBN 0-07-017864-X (pbk.) :
   1. Selling.   I. Yeager, Joseph C.   II. Sommer, Linda.
III. Title.
HF5438.25.D76   1991
658.8'5 — dc20   91-3464
                                                            CIP

ISBN 0-07-017865-8 {HC}
ISBN 0-07-017864-X {PBK}

1 2 3 4 5 6 7 8 9 0   DOC/DOC   9 8 7 6 5 4 3 2 1

*The sponsoring editor for this book was Betsy Brown, the editing supervisor was
Marion B. Castellucci, and the production supervisor was Pamela A. Pelton.
This book was set in Baskerville. It was composed by McGraw-Hill's
Professional Book Group composition unit.*

Printed and bound by R. R. Donnelley & Sons Company.

*This book is dedicated to the memory of
Jane Drozdeck
—a great lady who is
much loved and appreciated.*

*This book is also dedicated to the
extended families of Steve, Joe, and Linda
who give us their love and support. Special
mention should be made of Sandy, Nick, Ben,
Rachael, and Jerry.
We truly appreciate you all.*

*Finally, this book is dedicated to
you, the reader. Your pursuit of
excellence will make the world
a better place.*

Contents

Preface

You have just opened a powerful and effective book on persuasive communication which consolidates the techniques presented to over 20,000 people at companies such as Merrill Lynch, Pfizer, and Mercedes-Benz, to name only a few.

What They Don't Teach You in Sales 101 is designed to give you leverage in your pursuit of sales success. Thousands of our students have doubled and tripled their production because they learned the essential patterns of influence underlying human communication and the characteristics shared by especially successful people. You, too, will learn to use many of the techniques perfected by some of the most renowned communicators in the world.

If you have ever lost a sale, you can be sure something happened that you were not aware of—otherwise you would have made the sale. This means that the client was unique in some respect that escaped your notice. Traditional sales approaches and responses are normally geared to the "generic" prospect. Yet there is no such thing as a "generic" prospect. Each person is unique! We concentrate on the uniqueness of each individual and offer methods that make prospects want to become your clients—and as soon as possible. The difference between this and other sales books is that it provides the user with the nuts and bolts of communication. The message of this book is *results, not promises, count.*

Natural and Provable Techniques

Our approach is based upon natural psychological indicators which are easily seen and understood by anyone trained to notice them. By learning and applying these scientifically verifiable indicators, you will be assured of a high probability of success because you will be influencing others on both the conscious and unconscious levels of awareness. This book is designed to enhance your abilities by offering you special knowledge and skills which can be blended with those you already have.

Imagine if you could gather the top thousand professional communicators in the world in one location to learn what makes them so special. They would come from all areas of life: negotiators, salespeople, politicians, psychologists, advertisers, and so on. Imagine further that you could discover the common patterns, the "key" to communication of these professionals with completely different styles and personalities. Finally, imagine that you could learn to do what they do, and as well as they do it, while at the same time developing your own unique style. Would this be useful to you? These patterns have been identified and are taught in these pages!

Unconscious and Conscious Processes

Over the years, psychologists and other communication specialists have repeatedly demonstrated that 75 to 90 percent of all communication occurs below our conscious level of awareness and that only 10 to 25 percent of our decisions are made consciously. Most of our likes, dislikes, preferences, and reactions to people, places, and things are determined by unconscious mental processes.

Think about it. If you could exert considerable influence on the unconscious minds of other people, you would certainly become much more effective and powerful in virtually anything you do. You would have eliminated many of the random factors that contaminate most communication. Exactly how to accomplish this is taught here.

The Science of Communication

During recent years, discoveries have elevated the "art" of communication to the "science" of communication. These discoveries will help you understand how your words and actions will unconsciously and consciously affect other people. It has been repeatedly demonstrated that success in this world is partly based upon the ability to communicate effectively with others. Yet until now, no one has taught you *how* to communicate effectively.

We have combined our studies of neurolinguistic programming

(NLP) with many other highly effective communication techniques to provide you with a systematic, coherent approach to sales. This approach has significantly increased the productivity of thousands of salespeople, managers, and other professional communicators.

This book answers the question: "How, specifically, do individuals at the top of their professions consistently and elegantly achieve their results?" A meticulous study of great professional communicators in many fields has resulted in the development of a set of powerful, effective, and systematic tools of communication designed to help anyone in the communication or sales fields to achieve results easily, efficiently, and effectively.

A very significant finding was that there are two distinct approaches that must be taken to achieve the highest levels of success: (1) learning how to deal effectively with others including understanding how they think, react, and are motivated, and (2) learning how to condition yourself effectively for success by being enthusiastic, confident, and focused. *What They Don't Teach You in Sales 101* deals with both of these approaches in a very practical way.

For example, rapport is considered to be one of the key ingredients to any sale. Virtually every sales book we've ever read emphasizes the need to establish rapport because it is so crucial to selling and communication. Yet the techniques to gain rapport are usually described in vague terms such as "Be warm and responsive," "Let the prosepect know you really care," "Show that you're interested," and "Make them feel comfortable."

The question then becomes, "How, *specifically*, do you establish rapport with someone?" How do you prove it? How do you create chemistry, that special magic that appears between certain people? You will learn specific techniques to develop that chemistry with anyone.

You'll also learn a systematic approach to sales success. The chapters in the book provide a complete "package" that will give you the competitive edge.

The 2 Percent Differential Equals the 1600 Percent Difference

It has been repeatedly demonstrated that approximately 80 percent of the results (productivity, sales, cases won, etc.) are obtained by 20 percent of the people. This is the famous 80-20 rule that seems to apply to most industries and professions. This rule means that the top 20 percent of the performers—the stars—are producing at a rate 16 times greater than the average performer. These star performers are not 16 times more intelligent; nor do they have 16 times more ability or product knowledge; nor are they 16 times better than anyone else.

Since we know that one person is not 1600 percent better than another, the question is, "What is the difference that makes the difference?" We call it the 2 percent differential. This 2 percent represents minute, yet significant, differences in both the initial approach and the presentation.

These subtle modifications might be as simple as changing your rate of speech and tonal qualities, emphasizing certain words and phrases, using benefit statements based upon the client's bottom-line needs, or responding to the unconscious reactions that are continually being broadcast. Star performers make subtle, yet significant, adaptations to their clients. *These unconscious adaptations make all the difference in the world.*

What You Will Learn

Whereas standard sales books typically cover topics such as how to prepare for a sales call or how to qualify a client, *What They Don't Teach You in Sales 101* is designed to ofer new skills that can augment the know-how you already have. Below is a brief list of some of the things you will learn in this book. While reading the list, imagine a few of the ways that you will personally benefit from having this knowledge. You'll learn:

- How to establish, maintain, enhance, and if necessary, reestablish rapport with virtually anyone. You'll learn to attain a deep level of rapport in minutes instead of hours.
- How literally to match your presentation to the preferred thinking style of your client.
- How to neutralize resistance or hostility while getting information that will close the sale.
- How people think and process information. You will then be able to package your presentation accordingly.
- How to control what effect words have on a client.
- How to generate excitement and motivation in virtually anyone.
- How to use effective questioning techniques that increase your impact.
- How to discover the major buying motives of your clients. (Since each

person is different, we'll concentrate on how to discover and use the information to enhance your sales presentations.)

■ Much, much more!

By applying the techniques presented in this book, you will develop that special edge enjoyed by other star performers.

The Net Result

You'll be learning many techniques which will increase your knowledge of communication as well as significantly enhance your skill level. Each technique is a part of the whole. The cumulative effect is that you will greatly improve your persuasive abilities, which will assist you whenever you interact with other people. Good luck!

Steven R. Drozdeck
Joseph Yeager
Linda Sommer

Acknowledgments

Of the many people who contributed to our effort, we will single out a few for very special mention. They saved us many sleepless nights and repaired many of our little oversights. We thank Ed Rosner, who slogged through our original manuscript, as did Curt Broadway. Special assitance was also rendered by Jitu Shah, Ed Folk, Sang Shin, and Eleanor Clarkson. Of course, we thank the people who made us all possible: Steve's Mom and Dad, Linda's Mom and Dad, as well as Joe's Mom and Dad.

We also give a very special thank-you to Sandy Champion-Drozdeck who did some excellent fine-tuning to the final manuscript, contributed numerous ideas and energy, and was gracious enough to marry Steve.

Most people are unaware of how a book can be enhanced by its editors. We're grateful to Betsy Brown, Marion Castellucci, and Hilah Selleck for their efforts on our behalf. We also thank the publishers. If we have left anyone out, we thank you too.

Introduction from the Mentor

Throughout the book you will find commentary from a mentor. A bit of philosophy, a bit of wisdom, and some motivation are provided. The commentary also helps explain the material that follows. We think that you'll enjoy this approach. It allows us to discuss topics that merit your attention but do not merit entire chapters. It also allows us to tie together many of the concepts and techniques introduced in the text.

My friends, over the last 15 years I've worked with many, many sales-people. They've sold everything from socks to stocks, from cars to carpets, and from mainframes to picture frames. They've been from every age, creed, race, and political affiliation. Their backgrounds would be too varied to even attempt to describe. It has been my pleasure to work with over 20,000 people in small groups or one-on-one. I've learned a lot from them, and they've learned a lot from me.

I've been fortunate to personally interact with many of these people over the years and have been doubly fortunate to be able to interweave their information with that culled from hundreds of books on sales, management, communication, psychology, and philosophy.

In the pages that follow, you will learn some of the techniques that are the essence of effective persuasion.

Effective persuasion—an interesting concept, but what does it mean? It means gathering the resources available to you and presenting them to the client using verbal and nonverbal processes in a way that is meaningful to that individual. It means dancing to different music and with different partners. It means having the ability to say the same thing many ways so that you can deal with many different personalities, needs, and motivations. It means being able to be physically, mentally, and emotionally comfortable with virtually anyone and they with you. It means that

1

you can achieve the highest level of your profession and really make a name for yourself.

I know it sounds like a lot. In one way it is. In another way, you already do many of these things. However, most salespeople — for that matter, most people — do them randomly, inconsistently, and ineffectively. The professional salespeople that I've met and read about are extremely effective and consistent. They do certain things consistently right. They adapt their style to the needs of the individual across the table or at the other end of the phone. They feel good about themselves and their profession. They know where they want to go, what they want to do, and how they intend to get there.

These are some of the topics in this book. Each topic is important. Each needs to be given attention if you want to enhance your performance.

These topics require practice, thought, and experimentation. They require that you believe that you can become better than you are. Of course, the better you are, the more you realize that further enhancements are possible. Those who think they are already perfect never even venture beyond their own mental limits. You wouldn't be reading these words if you weren't a candidate for stardom.

Life is interesting. You get what you ask for and what you work for. But there is more to it than asking and working. Otherwise, everyone would be successful. You must really want it. Most people don't get what they want because they don't know what they want. This will be important for t!.e realization of your goals and dreams. You'll learn a lot about how other people think. You'll learn about what motivates other people and how to motivate them. As you learn about them, you'll also be learning about yourself. What makes you tick? What motivates you? What will maintain the burning desire to succeed? This information will transform your "I'd like to succeed" into a powerful force that cannot be denied.

All the desire in the world is useless if you do not have effective tools and techniques with which to transform that desire into reality. Knowing "how to" is as important as having the "want to." There are numerous techniques that you will learn which you'll undoubtedly find fascinating. Sometimes they are just common sense; sometimes they are new discoveries about unconscious thought processes. But they are always fascinating.

Yet there is one more thing that must be addressed: your willingness to implement many of these ideas. This is an important consideration because all of the academic knowledge in the world is worthless unless you are able to put it into practice. Some of these techniques will eventually become an automatic part of your behavior, but only if you practice.

Experiment! Try the techniques on for size! You have absolutely everything to gain and nothing to lose. However, you have a tremendous

amount to lose by not trying. It is a foregone conclusion that no matter what your sales and communication skill level is now, it can become better.
Here is one of my favorite metaphors:

Imagine that I am on a cruise ship and become involved in a Ping-Pong tournament. The score is 20–20, and it's my serve. If I make the shot, I win fame and glory. So I toss the ball and hit it with all my might in an attempt to make a grand slam, but the ball flies right into my opponent's forehead. Shame. Embarrassment. Laughter from the crowd. I lose.

Later, a Ping-Pong professional approaches me and comments that at the key shot, my wrist was bent during the serve and this caused the ball to have an upward spin, almost giving my opponent a frontal lobotomy. "Your wrist needs to be straight and the paddle held like this" is the pro's final comment.

"I'll never do that again!" I think and go about my business. Two days later, another game. The score is 20–20. My serve. Toss the ball into the air, hit it with all my might directly into my opponent's forehead.

If I were a professional, I would have been practicing nothing but my grand-slam serves during the interim. As a professional, I would have made sure my wrist was straight even if I had to tape a ruler to my wrist.

As an amateur, I merely thought about it and did not practice.

What do you want to be...an amateur? Or a professional? In sales, basically, you are a professional motormouth. Your success is based upon both the words you use and how you say them. A sales professional will practice.

You really need to create a habitual response to success. Let me end this commentary with one of my favorite quotations. It summarizes a lot of what was just said.

I am your constant companion.
I am your greatest helper or heaviest burden.
I will push you onward or drag you down to failure.
I am completely at your command.
Half the things you do you might just as well turn
   over to me and I will do them — quickly and
   correctly.
I am easily managed — you must be firm with me.
Show me exactly how you want something done
   and, after a few lessons, I will do it
   automatically.
I am the servant of all great people; and, alas, of
   all failures as well.
Those who are great, I have made great.
Those who are failures, I have made failures.

I am not a machine, though I work with all the
   precision of a machine, plus the intelligence of a person.
You may run me for profit or run me for ruin—
   it makes no difference to me.
Take me, train me, be firm with me, and I will
   place the world at your feet.
Be easy with me and I will destroy you.
Who am I?
I am Habit!

Keep this in the front of your mind as you go through the chapters. Remember, it is your choice. What do you want to be?

There are a number of other things which need to be said. I'll wait until a more appropriate time, either at the beginning of a particular section or interspersed throughout the text.

Meanwhile, I'm sure that you'll enjoy the book and will be able to put the techniques and ideas to immediate use.

Good luck and best wishes,

Your Mentor

PART 1
Prospecting

There are a number of things we have to discuss. Part of your concern has to be how to become even more productive than you are. This is reasonable and fair.

You've heard it before, and you'll undoubtedly hear it again. There are two ways to make more money: get more clients, or get more money from the clients you already have. Each of these requires two distinct sets of skills: excellent interpersonal communication skills and the perception that you are a professional.

As mentioned before, communication skills is what this book is all about. However, it is worth briefly commenting on being perceived as a professional. Think about yourself and your friends for a moment. You've gone shopping and have undoubtedly been approached by a number of salespeople. Some you liked, and some you probably didn't. Did you ever have an uncomfortable feeling with one of them? Perhaps it was his manner. Perhaps it was her clothing. Maybe the person just didn't fit.

Here is a question: Pretend that you asked a question about a stereo system that you were thinking about purchasing. Pretend that the salesperson said something equivalent to "I really don't know anything about it." Would you buy from that person? If the manager of the store gave you the same response, would you buy from that store? Unless you have specific knowledge about the product that you wished to purchase, the probability is that you would seek more professional assistance. You need to be comfortable with the vendors that you are dealing with. After all, if you are going to give them your hard-earned money, you want to know that they are competent.

There are many fine books which describe some of the elements you need to make an initial favorable impression. It has been suggested that an initial impression — good or bad — is made within the first 3 seconds. Whether this is fair is immaterial. How a person looks, talks, and acts contributes to how we feel about that person.

Fortunately, we can "package" ourselves to create the image we want to initially project. This package provides the first opportunity to influence others without their being aware of it. The next opportunity to positively influence a person occurs when we begin communicating.

There are only two ways to make more money in sales: get more clients and/or get more orders from the clients you already have. The next three chapters deal with generating more leads, generating enthusiasm from your prospects, and generating motivation within yourself to continue.

1
Generating
New Business

Most sales professionals wish to expand their business and compensation and are therefore constantly seeking new clients. Prospecting is the traditional method of accomplishing these goals.

The purpose of this chapter is to provide an overview of the prospecting process. In it, we'll discuss:

- Reasons for prospecting
- Finding hundreds or thousands of ideal clients
- Contacting people by phone and mail

Why Prospect?

When you prospect, you are developing a continuous source of new clients to further develop your business. Unless you are in a business in which prospecting is inappropriate or unnecessary, the need to bring in additional clients is essential. It gives you additional money, which is always nice to have. (People who have had experience with tax audits may debate the previous sentence.) Additional clients also allow you to maintain your current standard of living, which would otherwise be reduced because of client turnover. In many industries the rule of thumb is that you will lose 20 to 50 percent of your clientele each year because clients move, switch to the competition, die, become dissatisfied, or leave for other reasons. The income loss that you experience due to this turnover requires that these expected losses be replaced.

You can just sit back and wait for things to happen, or you can make things happen. Prospecting allows you to insert some control into your business. It allows you to progress beyond those who are complacent. Remember, "If you're not going forward, you're going backward."

Qualify the Client for You

When initially speaking to prospects, you are in a fact-finding process in which you are qualifying the client in two ways: Do they need you? Do you want them? Additionally, you are positioning yourself and them for a buying decision.

Prospecting Purpose 1: Do They Need You?

Can you and your company supply what they want or need? If not now, how about in the future? If the answer is no, then remove that person from your list of names. Before you do that, however, you have the opportunity for a referral and potentially for some cross-selling, both of which will be explained below in greater detail.

Prospecting Purpose 2: Do You Want Them?

When making prospecting calls one of your main purposes is to determine whether it is worth giving this person a follow-up phone call. While closely correlated with "Do They Need You?" this question goes further because you must also evaluate the time and effort needed to make this person or company a client. At this point you must be very bottom-line oriented. The prospect may only have a limited amount of money available yet demand a great deal of attention. The person may have an abusive personality, which makes dealing with them a psychic chore.

Because "time is money" you should devote your attention to those who are worth your while. Remember, there are thousands people who need your assistance. Why spend time with those who offer you little or no potential?

Evaluation of a prospect's potential is an ongoing process. From week to week, circumstances can change for you or for them. You must always make a determination regarding the most effective use of your time and energy. Remember that while you are talking to a low-probability candidate you are not contacting someone with even more potential.

Knowing when to let go is something that comes with practice and effective questioning. Newer salespeople tend to hold on too long. Experienced salespeople often let go too quickly. We've read reports that show how most new accounts are opened after the sixth phone call, whereas most salespeople stop after the third. This may be part of the reason that a relatively small group of sales professionals take home the majority of commission revenue.

Prospecting Purpose 3: Position for Buying Decisions

The final purpose of prospecting is to position those prospects for buying decisions. Through the use of the other skills described in this book and thorough fact-finding, you discover the person's criteria and hot buttons. Your subsequent sales presentations are more powerful, effective, and persuasive as a result of this knowledge. During this initial conversation, you also position yourself as the person who can meet their needs.

While determining their needs, desires, and motivations, you will also develop a very deep level of rapport (subject of Part 4) so that the person both likes you and wants to do business with you.

In summary, prospecting allows you to maintain and increase your level of income by adding to your client base. While there are numerous ways of making the first contact, the initial conversation allows you (1) to determine if they need you, (2) to determine if you want them, and (3) to position them for a purchase. Effective questions and rapport are a major part of the initial contact.

The effectiveness of this initial qualification process is partly dependent on the quality and quantity of the prospects you are contacting.

The Ideal Prospect

Who in the world would you most like as a client? Eliminating any billionaires or mere multimillionaires, think about the characteristics of your ideal client. You can pick virtually any economic level, background, or characteristic you can imagine. What prospects do other salespeople dream about having? As long as you stay within the bounds of reason, there are hundreds or even thousands of people who fit the majority of the characteristics that you want.

Part of the problem with some salespeople is that they try to go after anybody and everybody that has a dollar. While this may seem to be the most logical way of doing things, in reality, it is not as efficient as focusing your efforts, after your start-up period, in which it *is* logical to explore all avenues. Shortly thereafter you should become more and more focused as you pursue certain types of clientele. For example, a computer salesperson may begin by selling any type of computer possible to anyone wishing to buy but may find that some of her best clients are parents of school children. They refer other parents, which causes our saleswoman to become even more expert in computer-assisted learning. At that point, she may wish to devote more of her time and effort to this particular market.

Begin your prospecting efforts as if you were a strobe light. You want everyone to know that you exist and will pursue a variety of markets. As you obtain success with any particular group, devote more of your time and energy to similar prospects. As you become even more knowledgeable about a particular market segment, you become a recognized expert. At that point you have shifted from being a strobe light to being a laser beam.

Ideal Prospects by the Thousands!

The sources of names of potential prospects are limited only by your imagination. Depending on your industry you can use trade associations, church groups, owners of small pleasure craft, members of certain clubs, professional groups, etc. Again, depending upon the industry, you can find a wealth of information in your local newspaper and from the local court. Marriages, estates, and new business formations are only a few of the items commonly available from these sources. It may take some time to find out what is available, but once you do, you can hire a high school student to do the legwork for you. The more names of potential prospects that you have the better your probabilities. There are companies which, for a very modest price, will compile lists of thousands of people for you to contact via the telephone or the mail.

Consider asking your friends and family about ways of discovering new sources of business. They'll approach it from a different perspective and will often provide worthwhile ideas. Most people welcome the opportunity to make a contribution.

A secondary benefit is that they then become excellent sources of referrals. You have put their brain into gear to help you. Weeks after your initial discussion with them, they'll still be working for you and will apprise you of any opportunities. We know of numerous sales pros who have gotten substantial amounts of business in this way. It's one thing when you let your friends know that you would appreciate any referrals they have and something completely different when you engage their minds.

Also speak to the vendors and other suppliers of your business. They are often highly knowledgeable about your market and may have a few ideas that even your boss and senior sales associates haven't considered. If your firm has an operations department or a customer service department, consult with the experts in those divisions — they have to interact with the client on a different level and may offer a different point of view. One point, though: it may cost you a few lunches.

In essence, while there are thousands of potential prospects for your services, it is useful to enlist the minds of others in the search.

Once you have identified certain key characteristics, you can enlist the aid of professional data managers to quickly find names. Earlier we mentioned using students to do the legwork and to leverage your time, effort, and money. List companies may do it even more efficiently.

Using a Mail List Company Effectively

There are some important things to consider whenever you use a mail list company:

1. There are many list companies that have information about your area. Look in the phone book yellow pages under "Advertising — Direct Mail." However, be aware that:

2. The standard lists have probably already been used by others in your profession. However, you can quadruple the value of your list when:

3. You can create a personalized list that will find people who are very close to ideal prospects.

Think again of an ideal prospect, perhaps by thinking of the common characteristics of your current best clients. For example, you may want to search for people who are married and between 40 and 50 years old, own their own homes, take vacations by flying first class, have 2.3 children, and read a particular magazine. The list company can probably provide you with thousands of names of people who meet all or most of the criteria that you have established. You can be highly specific and selective. Create an ideal prospect and let the list companies find people who match *most* of the criteria.

Of course you have to pay for these supercharged lists. There is usually a slight, incremental charge for each additional criterion that you select. For instance, the list company might search for all the married couples and then cull and remove anyone who does not own a house.

From this smaller listing, they would eliminate anyone who is younger than 40 and older than 50, leaving a smaller list. They might then search the readers of whatever magazine(s) you selected. The process goes on and on until you have the names of a few hundred or thousand highly qualified individuals. You have just increased your efficiency because you can tailor your mailings to meet the probable needs of these people.

If you are too narrow in your focus, the list company will let you know that they cannot supply the quantity of names you requested. It is in their best interests that you are successful because you will then use their services again. As a result, if your selection criteria are too selective, they will help you modify your criteria. (There probably are numerous list companies that have what you need. Check with two or three companies. There is no reason that you must be limited to only one.) Often they will provide useful ideas that can be incorporated into your prospecting program—mail or phone.

Because your success ratio usually becomes significantly higher and your time and energy are being used much more productively, you are often reimbursed for the increased cost of the list within the first few new accounts. Although these supercharged lists may be about twice as expensive as ordinary lists, they pay for themselves. It reduces the randomness of selection by one additional factor.

Now you have hundreds or thousands of names of people who are high-probability candidates for you. You probably would want to call each person, but who do you call first? Not everyone on the list is equal. Some are going to be "more equal" than others. How do you know which is which?

Mail Them Something

Mail these prospective clients a letter to inform them of your product and offer them the opportunity to call or write for additional information. You would probably be wise to ask someone in your company's advertising department to help you compose a letter specifically designed to meet the needs of that select listing. Those who respond to your mailing are the people you contact first. You may have offered a free review of something, or a demonstration, or your willingness to be of service. Regardless of what you offer, the people who respond have some sort of immediate interest in you, your product or service, or something related. When you respond to their request, they will be appreciative and will probably do business with you.

The people who do not respond to the mailing can still be eventually called using the "Did you get my letter?" approach. For example,

"Mr./Ms. Prospect, last week you received a letter from me which..." At this point it is no longer an absolute cold call. Rather, there should be a degree of receptivity. You realize that the person probably didn't read the letter. That doesn't matter. Tell him about what the letter contained. At that point, you are qualifying the person with respect to your product or service.

Remember that you already know quite a bit about these people. Each one is highly qualified by inclusion on the list that you had tailor-made. The only purpose for the letter is to determine which members of the list are hot prospects. Try two or three variations on the same letter. Send out two or three hundred copies of each letter and find which one provides the best response. Then go with the best.

Referrals—Getting and Giving

Referrals are another excellent source of new business. If you ask for referrals often enough, you will get them. The beautiful thing about referrals is that you have a much more receptive person at the other end of the line. Most people are quite willing to provide assistance if asked nicely. For example, "I'm pleased that I was able to assist you and would welcome the opportunity to assist some of your friends or family members. Who in your (choose one) neighborhood/club/church/profession/family might I be able to contact?" While not everyone may give you a referral, you will be quite surprised at the number that you do receive.

The vast majority of star performers leverage their time and efforts by consistently requesting referrals from their prospects and clients—they realize that they have everything to gain and nothing to lose. Once requested, people tend to be on the lookout for people who have similar needs to their own. Once you contact a referral, you usually find them receptive because people usually take the advice of friends, and they run the risk of offending their friends by being short with you.

Make sure that you periodically thank the people and express your appreciation. People will do virtually anything for you if you are appreciative.

In essence, the idea behind prospecting is that there are usually many people out there who need your specific product or service. The trick is to ask questions and to keep your eyes and ears open to opportunities. Remember, if you want to increase your income or opportunities within the company, you must get more clients.

One of the funniest incidents regarding referrals happened to a stockbroker who was calling the president of a large manufacturing company. After the stockbroker finally got through to the president, the latter ranted and raved about how he had lost money in the stock market and that all brokers were crooks and made a host of similar statements. The broker allowed the client to vent his anger and, because he had nothing to lose, asked for a referral. The president, of course, would not give the broker the names of any friends or associates because he believed that brokers would merely lose their money. "Give me the name of your biggest competitor," said the broker, "so I can lose his money." The president provided the name. The broker then called the competitor and related the entire story. The competitor, after a good laugh, opened an account. The broker then called the original person back to thank him for the referral. The president was so intrigued with the broker that he also opened an account.

Giving Referrals

During the course of your day-to-day conversations you will undoubtedly discover needs that you cannot fulfill. Rather than saying, "Sorry, I can't help you," say "I know someone who may be able to help you. Would you like his/her name? (for him/her to give you a call?)" If you have developed a list of contacts, you become a center of influence. "One hand washes the other." It is another way of maximizing your effectiveness. Make sure your client uses your name when contacting this other person. Also, send this person a note indicating you gave his name. He may reciprocate by giving your name when appropriate.

While mailings, referrals, phone calls, and seminars are all effective approaches, each becomes more viable when used with other approaches. Regardless of the particular method that you use, there will come a time that you actually speak to the prospect for the first time. What you say and how you say it become important as you generate prospect interest — the subject of the next chapter.

2
Initial Statements to Generate Interest

In the previous chapter we mentioned that you can initially contact someone by letter and then follow up by phone. If you are fulfilling a request, your initial statement could be as simple as, "Last week you asked for information on_____. I'd like to answer any questions that you may have." Even though they didn't read it, they are under a social obligation to be civil to you. Responding to client requests is the easiest of the follow-up calls.

Any mailing that you had done served to identify which 1 to 3 percent of the prospects you should contact first. Now comes the decision regarding what to do about the vast majority (97 to 99 percent) of the people who did not respond to the mailing. (A 2 to 3 percent response on a mailing is generally considered good.) Do you contact them or not? Remember that these people are probably in need of your services. It cost you time, effort, and money to get their names. It would be rather expensive to discard the list.

The most logical alternative is to give them a call. Herein lies your challenge. How can you get the person interested, quickly and consistently?

20 Seconds to Get Their Attention

When you are prospecting by phone, you usually have only 10 to 20 seconds to say something that is interesting and exciting and which causes the prospect to want to hear more. Depending upon the background information that you already have, this can become rather simple. Businesspeople like to know what their competitors are doing. People generally like to hear what other people are doing.

Your initial statement should include solutions that would probably appeal to the individual that you are speaking with. For example, if you know that the person has a child in high school (you could have created a list that includes this as a criterion), you would have a higher level of receptivity if your initial statement included something that would appeal to people in this situation. For example, "The costs of higher education are becoming enormous. If I could show you a way some of those costs could be offset, would you be interested?" (You already know that this is a probable concern.)

The prospect can answer either yes or no. In either case your next question is "Why?" This question has a good probability of getting them to talk. Their response will further qualify them regarding your product. Even if there is no need, in which case you have limited the amount of time and effort you have spent, you can ask for a referral.

Also remember that one of the primary purposes of prospecting is to determine if you ever wish to speak to this person again. If they disqualify themselves for your product or service, you have merely come one step closer to a sale with someone else. One way of thinking about sales is that you are paid to get through all of the initial rejection so that you can make the sale. And the more rejection you get, the better you feel.

After you get their attention, you want to get them talking. There is an old adage that "no one ever hung up on themselves." As they talk, you are obtaining the information that you need. Through the use of effective questioning techniques (taught in Part 2), you can direct the conversation to gain the additional information that you need to close the sale.

Elements of an Opening Statement

Essentially, the initial opening statement should be personal and specific, aggressive but not threatening, a disarming agent, and tailor-made for each group. The primary purpose is that the prospects should understand that they will receive a benefit from dealing with you.

You may as well think of your job as interrupting people for a living. In reality, there are very few people out there who are sitting by the telephone saying to themselves, "I sure hope a salesperson gives me a call today." They were doing something else when you called. Your call may or may not be a welcome diversion. Having an effective initial opening increases your initial positive response rate.

The following generic opening will give you the basic idea: "Hello, Mr. Prospect. My name is Mary Smith with XYZ Inc. Many of your neighbors are requesting information on our product because of its numerous advantages for people in your situation. Would you like to hear some more?" Granted, this is too generic to be useful, but it does show the structure in that it introduces the salesperson and the product, provides a probable benefit, and stimulates curiosity.

A car dealer might call families with children regarding a station-wagon or minivan. Rather than wait for the customer to come to them, they go to the customer. They purchase a list of people who subscribe to camping, hunting, or fishing magazines and then offer off-road vehicles. The salesperson would initiate a conversation with a topic related to the prospect's interest, thereby increasing the probability of a positive response.

The prospect has basically only two responses: yes or no. Regardless of their answer, your next question is, "Could you tell me why?" As they answer the question, they are basically qualifying themselves with respect to your product. Remember that the purpose of this first conversation is to determine Do they need you? and Do you want them? and to position yourself for a purchase. If they are unqualified, politely ask for a referral, get off the phone, and go on to the next person on the list. If they are qualified, you will continue the conversation, answering any questions that they have, while simultaneously gaining rapport. Your next step may be to send them additional information or to arrange a meeting.

Work with friends, associates, or someone from your marketing department to create a catchy opening statement. Often you can get a great idea by carefully reviewing your company's advertising program as well as those of your competitors.

However, regardless of the effectiveness of your initial opener, you will still regularly experience initial stalls and objections.

Stalls and Objections

Most initial prospecting calls result in the prospects' automatic defensive mechanisms coming into play. People are conditioned to react defensively. The most common example I know is what happens when a clothing store clerk asks if you need assistance. The almost universal, automatic response is "No, I'm just looking" or something similar. In a similar way, because of the many unprofessional phone calls that we are constantly bombarded with, most people will respond to sales calls in the negative.

Remember that this automatic response is merely a put-off, an initial stall. It does not necessarily indicate a permanent no, nor is it a rejection of you as a person. You have two choices at this point. Hang up the phone and try someone else or try to respond to that initial stall. The first alternative is promoted by some motivational speakers who suggest that success is assured to those who persistently call and constantly dial the phone. While this is true, it is not as efficient as attempting to respond to or bypass the initial barriers, thus creating your own successes rather than merely accepting the stall.

Handling Stalls: Increase Your Effectiveness

Assume that only 1 of every 10 people who hear from you has an immediate interest and that 9 of 10 respond negatively. If you try to overcome the initial objection, you will probably qualify an additional 2 people from the 9. Now you are qualifying 30 percent of the people you contact instead of only 10 percent. Over thousands of phone calls, this becomes significant. Over the course of 10,000 prospecting calls, which is what many salespeople make annually, qualifying 3,000 people versus 1,000 people gives much better probability. Some of those additional 2,000 people are going to become good clients. Of course, the other alternative is to make an additional 20,000 phone calls and consistently qualify 10 percent of those people. (Salespeople taking the latter course are encouraged to have their finger calluses removed regularly.)

Regardless of the specific product, service, or industry, the idea of attempting to respond to stalls and objections remains the same—you increase the number of people you qualify.

Handling Stalls: Potential Responses

Here are some typical stalls with some standard responses. They work partly because you have an immediate comeback which takes the prospect's comment into consideration. They should be previewed, modified to meet your individual style or situation, and then practiced so that you have an automatic response to automatic stalls.

> STALL: No money. *or* Not interested.
>
> RESPONSE: The chances of my calling you at a time when you have money available for an immediate investment in_____ product are rather remote. The reason for my call is to find out if we can establish a relationship for the future.
>
> RESPONSE: (not *designed to win friends and influence people, but we thought you'd get a chuckle from it*) Is this a permanent or temporary condition?
>
> STALL: Been burnt/hurt by your product/service/company before.
>
> RESPONSE: I'm sorry to hear that. What happened?

People sometimes need to vent their anger or frustration. While they review the situation, you are gathering valuable information about what they consider important. They usually feel good that someone listened to them and often appreciate you in the process. Remember that you are part of the solution, not the problem. You are only part of the problem if you don't listen.

> STALL: Already have another agent.
>
> RESPONSE: Many of our current clients *had* another agent before they began working with us. I'd like the opportunity to earn a portion of your business. *or* Many people in your situation have more than one agent. If I gave you an idea that made sense — would you buy it from me?

The key to overcoming stalls and objections is never defend, never explain. You are readdressing or redefining the question. Realizing that many responses are purely automatic, you will find it worthwhile to go to the next step. You are trying to ask the question "Are you potentially interested in how I can help you?"

There are undoubtedly other typical stalls which are standard for your profession. Make a list of of the ones given in the next 100 phone calls you make. After 100 calls you will have heard it all and have a response to virtually everything. When someone does offer something new, you can honestly say, "That's interesting. I've never heard that comment before. Can you tell me why you said that?" Once they start talking, you achieve your objective of qualifying them.

While you will qualify many additional people because you are willing to go the next step, you will still get a significant number of "No. Not interested" responses. The ability to continue searching for those who do need your product or service while disregarding the numerous negatives that you will receive is what salespeople are paid to do. If all you had to do was take orders you would have substantially less earning potential.

Remember that while we are suggesting that you respond to their automatic responses, we are not suggesting that you become a punching bag. You will significantly increase your success ratio if you realize that these things will happen and plan for them. You can almost make a game out of it. Since 9 of 10 people will have an automatic defensive response, try to figure which one they will use. Search for a new and better comeback. Try different ways. Have fun with it.

One of the most important characteristics of success is the stick-to-it-iveness of the star salespeople. They demonstrate a dogged determination to succeed. They keep on pushing. They keep on working even when they've had it up to their ears with difficult prospects and clients. What keeps them going? They seem to have more energy than the less successful salespeople and are often in much better physical shape. There are many reasons. One of the main ones, in my opinion, is that they realize the value of their time and they maximize their effectiveness. They also realize the value of each call that they make.

3
Keeping Yourself Going

When most people first get into sales they are filled with energy and have every intention of setting the world on fire. Their level of enthusiasm is a pleasure to behold. The first few prospecting calls might be intimidating, but people generally get the hang of it rather quickly. They become more efficient with time and practice and attention to small details.

The day-to-day hassles of the business tend to dampen a person's enthusiasm. Constantly dialing the phone and getting rejected by faceless people can take its toll on anyone. I understand the feeling. It's tough. There are, however, a number of things that you can do to help maintain your personal motivation.

Dialing for Dollars!

It is often wise to think about prospecting from different perspectives. Here is a perspective which has assisted hundreds of salespeople to maintain high levels of motivation. It can make cold-calling pleasant rather than distasteful.

Assume for a moment that it takes 10 phone calls to get a prospect and 10 prospects to get 1 client. This means that 100 phone calls must be made to get 1 new client. Also assume that each new client generates $100 in commissions.

Here's the key question: "If someone gave you a $1 bill every time you dialed the phone, how many times a day would you be willing to pick up that receiver?" In this example, it doesn't matter if you speak to a person; get a wrong number, busy signal, or no answer; or speak to someone and get a yes or no. Regardless of what happens, every time you pick up the phone and dial a number you receive $1. How many times a day would you try? Five? Fifty? One hundred? Three hundred? We've posed this question to thousands of salespeople, and most of them indicate that they would be able to make quite a few phone calls and feel good about each one. Furthermore, they would look forward to the next day's work.

While it is doubtful that someone would actually stand over you and physically hand you a dollar for each phone call, this is essentially what is happening when you dial for dollars. This truism makes the task of prospecting substantially more palatable. *You can give yourself a dollar every time you pick up the phone.* Some people mentally imagine that money is coming into their pocket whenever someone says no or hangs up. That mental picture negates the negative feeling that other salespeople might have. Some sales pros actually have a small kitty and physically move a coin from one pot into another. It makes it easier to realize that they are getting paid to make phone calls—not just for an occasional sale.

If you think about it this way, prospecting becomes much more enjoyable. Some people actually start to look forward to the 99 turndowns because they realize that it merely brings them one step closer to their goal.

How much do you make per call? You can compute it using the tally sheet presented next. After keeping track of your results for one or two weeks, determine how many phone calls or how many letters it takes to generate a prospect. How many people did you have to contact to get a commission? Divide the commission by the number of phone calls needed to get it, and you arrive at your current "income per phone call." Of course, this figure can be raised by applying the knowledge from this book.

An alternative computation is to take your weekly salary or draw and divide by the number of prospecting calls you make to figure out your income per telephone call. It doesn't matter that your manager is not physically standing over you. Making calls is what you are being paid to do.

As you increase the value and specificity of your list and as your skill level increases, you are increasing your own salary. We know many who have quintupled their per-phone-call value. You can too.

How to Measure Your Effectiveness with Prospects

If you keep a daily tally sheet of the number of dials, number of people reached, number of people that you qualified, number of accounts or sales that you made, and average commissions generated on each sale, you will be able to measure your effectiveness. Keeping a daily tally is a good idea because you can measure your level of efficiency in a number of ways. The tally sheet could look something like this:

Number of dials: ЈШ ЈШ ЈШ ЈШ ЈШ ЈШ ЈШ ЈШ ЈШ ЈШ = 50

People reached: ЈШ ЈШ ЈШ ЈШ ЈШ = 25

Qualified prospects: ЈШ ЈШ = 10

New Accounts: I

Commissions: $200.00

This tally sheet can be analyzed in a number of ways to measure the relative efficiency of your efforts:

- It took 50 dials to reach 25 people. This 2 to 1 ratio is excellent for most prospecting efforts—evidence of an excellent list. A ratio of 5 to 1 would also be considered good, while a ratio of 20 to 1 would indicate that you probably need to change your prospecting list or the time at which you are trying to contact the people on the list. A regular evaluation would allow you to immediately determine the effectiveness of your prospecting list.
- Being able to qualify 10 of the 25 people is also excellent. Usually the figures are significantly less. You would immediately realize that the list you were using was bad if your qualifying ratio dropped significantly from your average.
- Opening one new account generated $200 in commissions. Assuming that this was an average day, this salesperson was earning $4 for each call made—not bad for dialing the phone.

This periodic analysis alerts you to things that are going right or things that are going wrong. You are able to immediately see how you are performing and promptly take any remedial actions you think necessary.

How to Measure Your Effectiveness with Clients

A similar idea can be used with current clients. You can keep track of the:

- Number of calls to and from clients each day
- Number of clients reached
- Number of sales presentations made
- Number of times you asked for the order
- Number of sales
- Total commission revenue

The tally sheet might look something like this:

Number of dials: JHr JHr JHr JHr JHr = 25

People reached: JHr JHr JHr= 15

Presentations made: JHr JHr = 10

Order requested: IIII = 4

Order obtained: II = 2

Commissions: $1,200.00

Again, a regular tally would allow you to analyze your performance and determine where your efficiency level could be increased. Make special note of the number of times you actually ask for the order. We have found that many salespeople make the calls but never ask for the order. If you were to make note of it in the manner just suggested, it would become obvious. In the above example, the salesperson made 10 sales presentations but only requested an order 4 times. If this were a normal occurrence, it would have to be addressed further.

If the tally sheet showed many client contacts with few presentations, the figures would indicate that the salesperson was overservicing the clients.

One of the good things about keeping some sort of tally sheet is that you can make note of long-term changes. As you become even better, you will get a good feeling as you see your income per call steadily increase.

Think of your prospecting efforts as a machine. The constant monitoring will let you know when you have high performance and when you need tune-up.

Always remember, "Prospecting is a numbers game. The more people you dial, the more you succeed." You are literally dialing for dollars.

There are many other things that you can do to maintain your enthusiasm. One of the most effective is setting daily goals which allow you to become regularly successful.

Success through Daily Goals

We both know that to get the good things from this life there is a price that must be paid. The reward that you get can be happiness, because don't you just love it when you have a really successful day? The psychological reward certainly makes the effort totally worthwhile. The question is, how do you get more of these successful days? Success breeds itself. The more successful you are, the more successful you will become in a never-ending cycle of personal reward.

Yet just what is success? I think that Paul Meyer, the founder of Success Motivation Institute, said it best when he defined success as "the progressive realization of worthwhile, personal, predetermined goals." There's a lot to this particular definition that may not immediately meet the eye. Let's examine that definition more completely.

"Success is a progressive realization..." means that it comes in steps. Success isn't something you eventually attain, it's something that you are. You are successful each day that you reach your goals. It's the same thing with prospecting. Maintaining a base level of production, though, violates the need for a "progressive realization" of your goals. Being "comfortable" means that you've stopped progressing and started regressing. Remember that you will have client turnover and that, if you're not going forward, you're going backward.

The goals also have to be "worthwhile and personally meaningful" to you. Most people say that money is both worthwhile and personally meaningful. Yet it is the extremely rare individual who is motivated solely by money. Rather, most people are motivated by the things that having additional money can do for them. Money allows you to go on vacations; it allows you to enjoy some of the nicer things in life with those you care about. It is meaningless in and of itself.

There are things in life you can change and things that you cannot affect. You cannot, for instance, change the number of people that walk into your office today; you cannot change the economy or the amount of discretionary income that a person has. You cannot even change whether a particular person makes a purchase. But, you *can* make x number of mailings and y number of phone calls and ask for z number of referrals. You can realize that sales is a numbers game and that if you work the numbers you will eventually reap the reward. If you make your phone calls, you can feel good about yourself even if nobody was home. If you ask for z referrals, you can feel good knowing that today's response is merely a tiny part of what will occur this month. You therefore can pat yourself on the back and feel good. The next day, you are refreshed and ready to go, while other people are feeling sorry for themselves.

Perseverance is the key to success. President Calvin Coolidge made the point elegantly when he said:

Press on. Nothing in the world can take the place of persistence. Talent will not: Nothing is more common than unsuccessful men with talent. Genius will not: Unrewarded genius is almost a proverb. Education alone will not: The world is full of educated derelicts. Persistence and determination alone are omnipotent.

You have received a number of good ideas. It is up to you to implement them. Remember, "The difference between running and ruining a business is i."

PART 2
Understanding People

Throughout history certain people have controlled the destinies of kings and nations. They have had many titles and descriptions: wizard, power behind the throne, chief of staff, adviser, center of influence, statesman, and many more. They were the key opinion makers, the primary influencers, the master communicators of their times. Their opinions were always sought and carefully considered. Sometimes they had even more power than those they served.

What made them so special? To a large extent, it was their ability to understand people and, therefore, situations. They intuitively knew how someone would probably react in a given situation. They understood how people thought and how they were motivated. This knowledge, combined with excellent persuasive skills, made them highly valued throughout the ages. This is still true today.

Understanding how people think and react is probably the most important knowledge you will ever acquire, because with it you can accomplish everything. "People skills" are highly valued in all societies. A premium is paid for such abilities. Understanding what drives behavior is key to the concept.

Yes, we are driven by conscious and unconscious forces which are extremely powerful. These forces drive people to success or failure, motivation or lethargy, love or hate, and are responsible for virtually everything *we do or fail to do. As you learn about others, you also learn about yourself.*

Think about it. If you could know what drives or motivates a person, you would be able to package your presentation in such a way that it is highly appealing to that person. They would like your idea because it would fit into their mode of thought, their unstated desires, their game plan. They would respond positively to you and to anything you said. This gives you a lot of power and an equal amount of responsibility to do "the right thing."

As you read this section, remember: "People do things for their reasons, not ours." The question becomes, "How do you know their reasons?" Read on.

4
What Makes Us Tick?

Persuasion

Persuasion is the discovery of another person's needs, wants, and desires and then the presentation of a solution which will satisfy those desires. Persuasion takes into account not only what the customer says but the probable reason he says it. For example, a person may state that he purchased a Mercedes Benz because of the quality and safety of the car; however, his real reason may have been to demonstrate to everyone he knows that he is successful. In this case, the socially oriented reason is equally or more important to the sales process than the stated reason.

Stated and Unstated Reasons

It is important to realize that the vast majority of people will usually have "hidden" or unstated needs, wants, and desires that are the actual motivations driving that person. They may think of them as likes and dislikes, or preferences.

Effective selling requires that you understand why people behave as they do and what motivates them positively and negatively. We will briefly examine the foundations of human behavior which form the basis of most sales and management courses. This information gives you a powerful edge. Your knowledge about how people think and react will be superb. You'll be able to anticipate their probable responses and to more effectively present your ideas.

Think of People You Know

As you read this material, it may be helpful to think of people that you have met that fit into each of the categories. If you can't think of a particular person, it would be helpful to think of television plots or characters which represent the various types. As you will shortly realize, the various descriptions represent key, or dominant, themes in our society. We are individually and collectively molded by the society just as societies are molded by the primary needs of the people. Your ability to recognize and flow with the key forces of human nature will allow you to more effectively influence and persuade.

Hierarchy of Needs

Abraham Maslow was a behavioral scientist who suggested that people behave in accordance with real or perceived needs. The following is an overview of Maslow's Hierarchy of Needs:

Basic

Protection

Social

Recognition

Self-actualization

According to Maslow each person has a hierarchy of needs which must be met. Once the key Basic needs (food, clothing, and shelter) are met, an individual becomes concerned with Protection issues as he or she seeks to protect and maintain the Basic needs. Once assured of Protection, Social needs become more important. The need for Recognition is the next step on the ladder, followed by the need for Self-actualization.

While rarely distinct steps, the position of a person on this hierarchy will often determine how he or she will react in a particular situation. It will often determine what will be motivating or persuasive.

Application of Maslow's Hierarchy
to People in the United States

Basic Needs.   While the majority of people in the United States and the other developed nations have their Basic needs taken care of, there are many who are homeless and wondering where their next meal is coming from. Approaching these individuals with the idea that they'll be "first on the block" would be futile.

Protection Needs.   The need for protection extends to business decisions. For example, the sale of a computer system to a department manager was made because the saleswoman pointed out that the purchase of a system made by a very well known manufacturer would never be questioned even if something went wrong with the system. Even though another manufacturer had a better product, the manager chose the "safe" purchase because he was uncomfortable about "sticking his neck out." Essentially, his insecurity in the job forced him to use judgments that were career protection–oriented.

So you see, if a person is in danger of losing property and/or a job so that his or her ability to provide food and shelter is in jeopardy, other things seem unimportant. Your awareness of your clients' dominant concerns will allow you to address their needs more appropriately. By indicating how your product will allow them to keep or protect what they have, you will be able to more effectively persuade them.

Social Needs.   Once Protection needs are satisfied, Social concerns take on greater and greater importance. Most people become members of some group. Social relationships, therefore, become a greater concern. Peer pressure and styles become key determinants in the decision-making process. These people will use the pronouns *we* and *us* often. Sales pros appealing to these needs by saying "your friends are doing the same thing," "everyone is doing it," or "do the 'in' thing," etc., have increased their probability of making the sale. By relating the product features, benefits, and advantages to the social realm, the astute sales pro has more effectively persuaded the customer.

Recognition Needs.   After satisfying their need to belong, the desire to rise in the pecking order is the normal next step. Recognition needs supercede the need to be merely a member. Gaining the respect of others becomes a dominant theme as the person increases self-worth. A salesperson would rephrase the advantages of his or her product or service to take this fact into consideration. "Your friends/associates will really admire you" becomes a very powerful sale point.

Self-actualization Needs.   Once esteem needs begin to be satisfied adequately, the need for Self-actualization becomes more prominent. "Feeling good about yourself" is a phrase which would make sense to such people. In a sales situation, for example, the astute sales pro might emphasize that "a Jeep will allow you to be who you are" or that a particular course will allow you to expand to your full potential. Either of these would meet the client's need to feel good about himself or herself.

Application of Maslow's Hierarchy to Sales

While the above information is interesting, the practical use of it, as well as the blending of each, will become more apparent with the following example:

A savings account paying high interest would appeal to each level in different ways. Making sure that the income will give enough money for food and rent will appeal to those Basic people who are on limited incomes. Using words and phrases such as "safety," "security," and "continuity of income" would appeal to people not only on the Basic level but those at the Protection level as well because this additional income will reassure the latter that they will be able to maintain their standard of living. However, asking these people to withdraw money for a purchase could be a scary proposition.

People at the Social level, whose base income is already secure, will positively respond to additional income in order to participate in group activities and would also like the idea that their friends are doing the same thing. Being "looked up to" appeals to the Recognition level. These people could be persuaded by indicating that "your clothing/car/lifestyle will set the standard for the rest of the group," or "people will look up to you as knowledgeable." Having the income to allow you "to do your own thing" appeals to to the Self-actualization level because it "would allow you to travel, take courses, or do virtually anything you want."

A person's interest in a product would be dependent upon whether the salesperson explained the need in terms that made sense based on that person's level. Telling a person who has Protection as a primary concern that "you can do your own thing" is meaningless and probably counterproductive to the sale. Of course, the customer may mentally transform what you said into something personally meaningful, but the salesperson hoping for this would be relying on luck. The sales professional takes as many things into consideration as possible, thereby decreasing reliance on luck while increasing the efficiency of skills.

In summary, by making note of a person's probable key needs you can increase the impact of your presentation by more precisely targeting the individual. All of the courses teach that benefit selling should allow the customer to understand the features, benefits, and advantages in terms that are meaningful to him.

While Abraham Maslow presented a psychological model which categorizes and explains many behaviors, it should only be thought of as a foundation from which additional refinements can be made. The concept of Power—Affiliation—Achievement coexists with Maslow's ideas.

Power—Affiliation—Achievement

There was some interesting research conducted by David McClelland, a professor at Harvard University. His studies of the "urge to achieve" for over twenty years have resulted in the "Power—Affiliation—Achievement" approaches of human motivation. You will find this applicable in many situations of your life. Again, it would be helpful to think of friends, associates, or family members that evidence some of the attributes presented here.

You can think of people as having one of three primary themes governing their behavior: the need for Power, the need for Affiliation, or the need for Achievement. Each of these results in certain overall responses which allow us to both predict behavior and motivate people based upon their demonstrated psychological needs.

Need for Power

The need for power is demonstrated in people who have a desire to control others and/or situations. They want things done their way or want other people to follow their directions. They want to build an empire. They are motivated by good reputation or position in the family, organization, or community; status; ability to influence others; ability to direct, supervise, and control; or ability to compete against and dominate others. Their favorite pronouns are *I, my,* and *me.* Words and phrases favored by power-oriented people are *control, power, authority, do it my way, that's my decision to make,* and *I'm the boss.*

To effectively influence the power-oriented person:

■ Acknowledge their status, position, and authority.

- Ask for their advice.
- Give them full credit for what they do.
- Let them believe it was their idea even if it was yours.
- Recognize them publicly.
- Let them know that they have influenced you.
- Keep them up to date on all developments.

They like to be in charge. It is their decision. Salespeople are advisers. Use the word *you*, with a slight tonal emphasis, rather often. (However, total reliance on *you* could be counterproductive because power-oriented people also respect those who are somewhat assertive.) The way to work with a power person is by empowering him or her.

Need for Affiliation

The need for affiliation is demonstrated by people who want to be associated with other people. They are motivated by a social orientation. They like to participate as part of a team, need to be liked, need acceptance and positive interpersonal relationships, like to work with others, like to minimize conflicts. Favorite pronouns are *us* and *we*. Words and phrases used by the affiliated person are *let's get together, let's do something for…, group effort, togetherness, help others, people, associate,* and *social*.

To maximize your effectiveness with affiliation-oriented people you should:

- Demonstrate that you enjoy working with them.
- Recognize the importance of social interactions and be prepared to participate.
- Smooth over potential conflicts.
- Indicate how others will want to associate with them.

Need for Achievement

The need for achievement is demonstrated by people who are primarily interested in achievement and want a sense of personal accomplishment. They seek out challenging and/or competitive situations. Realistic and achievable goals are set. They set a standard of personal excellence. They are motivated more by competing against a challenge or standard than by competing against others; they set high standards of achievement and accomplishment, develop new and original ideas and applications, set long-range objectives, and plan for contingencies. They will work with others to get the job done. However, they could just as easily work alone.

Words and phrases used by achievers are *innovative idea, accuracy, let's consider the long-term results, planning, achievement, accomplishment, meet plans and objectives,* and *goals*.

Achievement-oriented people would probably have the greatest positive responsiveness if you:

- Recognize their achievements through words and/or awards.
- Encourage independent thinking.
- Demonstrate appreciation for their accuracy and planning.

Having read the previous information you have probably been able to relate many of these themes to situations that you are already familiar with. Even if you have only seen some of it as a plot on a television show, you can recognize that it affects a certain percentage of the population.

In conclusion, you have learned how people may respond to situations based upon dominant patterns in their lives. As you compose your presentation, incorporate the themes described above and you will enjoy even greater success.

The next chapter introduces some effective questioning techniques which will help you define a person's overall motives while giving you insight into their specific needs.

5
What
I Think
You Said
Is...

Can you think of what you will do later today? Will you go to a meeting or to dinner? Of course you can easily think of the answer. It is a simple matter of imagining your future. You might think of imagining your future as a common everyday experience. But some people cannot do this simple mental act. This is not a case of brain damage! The reason is that their native language does not have any way to express the idea of the future.

The Limits of Language

The limits of language are the limits of the mind. In this chapter you will learn how some of our daily expressions can either help or hurt us. You'll find why and how the following saying applies to us: "I know you understand what you think I said, but I'm not too sure that what you heard is what I meant." Additionally, you'll learn some questions whose answers provide significant insight into what really motivates your client. As in the previous chapter, you'll probably learn certain things about yourself. All of this information will help lead to a sale.

Knowing What to Ask

When probing for information that will lead to a sales close, it is all too easy to ask unproductive questions. *The key to probing is knowing what to ask.* Probing is a many-faceted issue and can involve layer after layer of meaningful information. Successful salespeople know that some lines of questioning are more productive than others. The trick is knowing what areas are productive and what to listen for.

Your Questions Are Determined by Your Objective

There are priorities in what you need to know, and these priorities will determine what questions you ask. For example, you need to know what it takes to satisfy the customer and how he or she makes a decision. Certain questions will assist this process. Yet if your initial purpose is to establish rapport, then other questions may be more appropriate. If you are probing for hidden agendas, then another line of questioning is required.

Ultimately, your purpose in asking questions is to gain enough information that you can tailor your presentation. Immediately following this comment are two very useful questions which provide a wealth of information about the real needs of the client. These questions almost bypass the conscious processes and go directly to what really makes the person tick.

Two Key Questions

The purposes of these questions are to discover what factors or criteria are being used to make a decision and what "gut-level" benefits the client will receive.

Question 1: "What do you want in a＿＿＿＿?"　　The missing word or words represent any product or service the client may be interested in. The questions, "What do you want in a *car*?" "What do you want in an *insurance policy*?" or "What do you want in a *sales representative*?" will each elicit one or more key items that are important to the person.

The answer usually indicates what the person wants in your product or service. While almost any product or service has a variety of features, benefits, and advantages associated with it, only one or two of them will be meaningful to the client. The answer to Question 1 lets you know what needs to be emphasized in your presentation. Of course, other things may also be important, but you will have maximized your chances of presenting to the primary need.

Occasionally, you'll have to clarify your question because the client may not have understood you. If so, merely restate the question to get this important information, for example, "What is the most important thing for you in a_____?"

At this point you will have gotten words such as *performance, reliability, protection, convenience,* etc. These are the words that spark the client's interest and will need additional clarification, as explained later.

The second question allows you to delve more deeply into the client's needs, wants, and desires.

Question 2: "And what would having _____ do for/mean to you?" The missing word or words represent the criteria discovered by the first question. It explores why the criteria are important, and the responses indicate the deeper-level motivation behind what the client wants. Later, in your presentation, your benefit statements will focus on how what you have to offer fulfills the client's real desires.

For example, two people might want "performance" in a car. You might discover that "performance" would allow one person to get quick acceleration in emergency situations—which is really a safety issue. Another person may want "performance" because the "other guys will be forced to eat my dust." This is significantly different from safety. In either case, you now have a better understanding of what drives this person (pun intended).

In summary, the two questions "What do you want in a _____?" and "What would having _____ do for you?" provide valuable information. You'll often find that the answers are also correlated to clients' motivations of Power, Affiliation, or Achievement. The Hierarchy of Needs provides another cross-reference. When you put it all together, you have a more powerful presentation.

Try the following experiment with some of your friends. Make note of the difference in response to these two questions: "What would you do with an extra $5,000 a month?" versus "What would an extra $5,000 a month do for you?" The difference is usually that the first question results in things, while the second question often provides insight into their personal motivations.

The balance of this chapter will explore six additional language patterns which will assist you in understanding your client as well as in making the sale. These language patterns are labeling, mind reading, authoritative statements, lost yardsticks, overgeneralizations, and impossibility words.

The Basic Processes of Language

There are three basic ways that language makes things confusing for the uninitiated. People delete, generalize, and distort information in certain ways that are predictable from the way the English language works. The professional persuader knows how to spot and use these inevitable features. When a client gives you negative responses, it is often due to patterns of thinking and language which limit his or her ability to positively respond to your suggestions. Fortunately, you'll often be able to counteract such limitations though astute questioning.

A Rose Is a Rose. Or Is It?

If I ask you to think of a rose I am likely to get any one of many possible responses. Some people see a red rose, others an old flame of the same name, some a yellow rose, and so on. The point is that a word will produce a different internal image or idea for each person. For instance, if a customer complains about "the service" on an office copier, you might think he is referring to an incomplete maintenance effort. He may mean that the response time is too long between his call for service and the arrival time of the service technician. Or he may mean that you don't personally take his phone call. To know what the word *service* means, you would have to ask for his definition, or you'll probably respond to the wrong issue. *Ask*. Remember: "If there is a chance of a miscommunication, it pays to ask."

Read a few lines about a common situation:

> A little girl was playing in the street of her neighborhood. She heard the bell of the ice cream truck. She stopped what she was doing and ran home for money.

What is going on in the story? When asking audiences, we find a general trend that the little girl wanted ice cream and ran home for money to buy it. However, that is an intuitive interpretation, since the idea is not explicitly stated in the story. It is a conclusion based on a personal assumption.

Intuition is one of our most vital personal resources. It lets us sense what is going on and what to do. Yet, to make sure that the little girl wants ice cream, you have to ask her. After all, the truck bell may have reminded her to go to the store to do an errand. Your intuition can be right, and it can be wrong. Even context can be an unreliable indicator of what is really going on in the other person's mind. The best way to test your accuracy is to verify with a question.

Words Are Labels

Just as context can prove unreliable, you'll find that words themselves are unreliable until you probe for the meaning. People tend to assume that everyone has the same meaning. As you will see, they don't. Occasionally, it becomes important to discover the specific meaning. For instance, compare the information obtained by Salesperson 1 versus that obtained by Salesperson 2. Which is more useful in future interactions?

> CUSTOMER: All I want from a salesperson is good service.
>
> SALESPERSON 1: You can rely on me for good service.
>
> CUSTOMER: I'll take your word for it. Don't disappoint me.
>
> SALESPERSON 1: You'll get the best I have to offer.

Now compare this with the second dialogue.

> CUSTOMER: All I want from a salesperson is good service.
>
> SALESPERSON 2: What specifically do you mean by good service?
>
> CUSTOMER: I want you to return my call within five minutes regardless of what you're doing.
>
> SALESPERSON 2: I am sure that I could return your call within one-half hour. Would that be okay?
>
> CUSTOMER: I suppose that will do just fine.

You'll certainly agree that the two examples will lead to very different outcomes. The probability that Salesperson 1 will meet the client's specific service need is virtually nil. She'll do the best job she can, feeling great about her effort, only to have the client be hot under the collar for having been disappointed or "lied to" again. The label *service* can mean entirely different things to different people. It is to your advantage, as well as the customer's, to get complete understanding. This customer may not have realized that a 5-minute response time is unreasonable. "After all, doesn't everyone know that *good service* means a 5-minute response time?"

Here are some other common situations:

"I need more information."

Rather than providing every piece of literature ever written, you would be better off to discover what type of information is needed.

"I want a proposal." or *"Put something in writing."*

Each company has different standards and criteria for evaluating proposals. If you spend a short amount of time determining exactly what is expected, you have a better chance of fulfilling the client's expectations. Otherwise, you are shooting in the dark.

Some words are more important than others. The main idea is to think about potential misinterpretations of key terms. If you make a promise, then it is wise to make sure the other person has the same understanding as you do. An extreme example is a typical legal document, where almost everything must be defined to ensure mutual understanding and compliance. While it would be detrimental to be that precise in normal interactions, there is a need for certain understandings.

The mythical Murphy of Murphy's Law would probably put it this way: "If something can be misunderstood, it will be misunderstood, resulting in the worst miscommunication possible."

Mind Reading—The "I Know What You Mean" Fallacy

If you've ever heard statements like "I know what you mean," "She should know what I want," or "He's disappointed in me," you have heard people making assumptions about understanding what is in the other person's mind. For someone to "know what I want," I have to have told him or her specifically and exactly what I want. To truly know that someone is "disappointed," I would have to ask. Even then, the word is relative to the individual. Here are some examples of statements based upon mind reading:

"They all know what the policy means." How do you know that? Even if they all read the identical words, most people would have different interpretations.

"Of course they know how to do that." How do they know it? Were they taught it?

"It's obvious to me they want to do this." How is it obvious? Are there different potential interpretations?

"Salespeople think they can get away with anything." Which ones?

Do they all think that? How do you know that? What do they think they can get away with?

Mind reading has caused more misunderstandings, disappointments, and grief than almost any other thinking pattern that I'm aware of. People are funny. They always assume that "other people should be aware of my needs without my having to tell them." Some people won't even give a hint as to their needs, yet will become disappointed or even angry that the other person was unable to become a psychic and just "know" what was necessary.

Assuming is basically the same as mind reading. One of the best definitions of assuming that I ever heard was that whenever you ass/u/me, you run the risk of making an "ass" out of "u" and "me." Remember that things are rarely black or white. They are usually various hues and shades of gray.

The key to what has been taught thus far is to get specific information and to avoid assumptions. Sometimes this is difficult to do. However, the rewards are certainly worth the effort. In sales, you cannot afford the risks of a miscommunication.

A great English poet by the name of Rudyard Kipling wrote a poem entitled "Six Serving Men." He indicated that questions preceded by one of the six "men" Who, What, When, Where, How, and Why will get you the answers you need to just about anything. Learn to use them. However, you must learn to use them carefully. Asking these or any other questions in an aggressive manner usually results in a confrontation. Be very, very careful about how you ask the question.

If you attempt to match the client's words to your meanings, you will lose time, the client's attention and rapport, and probably the sale as well.

The next two verbal patterns will also give you insight into how the person thinks, as well as the tools needed to neutralize any negative comment.

Who Says...?

Occasionally people will make a statement which sounds as if it were a rule locked in stone. Comments such as "It's unfair to have inconsistent pricing" indicate that there are rules or key criteria regarding "consistency" and "fairness" and, perhaps, correct "pricing" in this person's mind. Whether a rule is valid is immaterial to understanding its importance to this individual. There are basically two things that you can do if this were a concern expressed to you: (1) accept that this person has a rule and work with it, or (2) gently question the person regarding the source of the rule.

Alternative 1: Working Within a Person's Rules.   First remember that you have received very useful information regarding the structure of this person's thought processes. A definitive judgment has been made which limits the person's thinking outside the scope of the statement. This is similar to "there's a proper way to do things here," which suggests that only a specific set of procedures is acceptable. Other approaches might not even be considered by this person. In extreme cases, these people would be considered closed-minded.

Unless it is important to the sale, let people keep their opinions. When you promote your company, you would want to emphasize how your production process has been carefully considered and that all the rules have been consistently followed. This makes sense to this person. It matches how they think.

Returning to the example on "pricing," we would wish to emphasize that any inconsistency is an illusion. A complex formula or procedure is somehow in place which really makes the pricing rather *consistent,* given the various factors which must be taken into consideration.

It is important to emphasize that the truth should be told. If, as in this example, there is consistency, by all means let the client know. However, if the client is right, be careful about trying to overcome his concern using anything less than the truth. Is there a sale so important that you would put your personal integrity on the line? If so, then why not try to change the situation before it becomes a problem?

Far too many people take the expedient way. While a salesperson may make a particular sale, he or she will eventually suffer a damaged reputation. As in most professions, your reputation should be of paramount importance to you. A good reputation makes people want to work with you, while a bad reputation will drive away even your current customers.

Alternative 2: Questioning the Source of the Rule.   When a rule is counterproductive to your purposes, you may wish to *gently* ask the person about how that rule came into being. Your tonal quality should indicate interest or curiosity.

Typically, the answer indicates that the person believes it has always been that way or "That's just the way it is." While remembering to sound curious, you can try to find out if there are any exceptions. As you are doing this, the client is unconsciously challenging the validity of his or her own assumptions. More often than not, the original hard and fast rule becomes more flexible. Often, in just a few questions you have changed the situation while getting useful information.

Occasionally you'll discover that there is some formal procedure that must be followed. If so, then that is also useful information for you to know and respect. This becomes especially important when working within corporate structures.

Lost Yardstick

In this situation an unconscious, often invalid, comparison is being made and applied to the overall situation. There is an unspoken standard of evaluation or one or that you are not aware of.

Customer comments you may hear include "This is the best product," "These components aren't well made," and "The program is too expensive." While each statement may be true in a certain context, it is based upon an unconscious comparison of one or more factors that is then generalized to make the final statement.

Taking them one by one, let us briefly analyze how the comparisons are made. Again, when you do this with clients, you obtain information regarding both how they think and their buying criteria.

"This is the best product."   What is the basis of comparison? The best in what category? What are other competitive products that might be better in a particular instance? (Of course, if the client is saying these wonderful things about *your* product, you probably would wish to avoid using the question regarding the competition.)

"These components aren't well-made."   What specification did it fail to meet? What criteria are you using? (If you know what a person is examining, you can take that into consideration in future discussions.)

"The program is too expensive."   Too expensive in comparison to what? Is a quality-versus-cost comparison being made or is the client referring to the pure dollar value? The question "What would make it reasonably priced?" would let you know what concerns must be addressed or how your proposal needs to be modified (assuming, of course, that it can be changed). Like almost everything else, *too expensive* is a relative term. Once you have the information, you have something to work with. Psychologically, once the client begins answering, the issue of expense is mentally reopened for reevaluation, that is, it is no longer a closed issue.

Two additional verbal patterns will be briefly introduced below regarding people who overexaggerate and those who are impossibility thinkers. You have undoubtedly encountered such patterns with regularity and probably found that they occasionally interfere with a sale.

Overgeneralization

"Every time I have *ever* bought *anything* from them, I was *totally* disappointed with *everything* I received." This is an extreme example of someone who overgeneralizes. They use words which are all-inclusive such as *every, all, never,* etc. The probability that no item that they ever purchased in their entire lives had a single redeeming value is rather remote. Yet in their thinking at that moment they distorted one or two situations and blew them out of proportion.

The key to dealing with this situation is to ask questions to find a single exception to break the rule. Even if there is just one exception, the rest of the house of cards quickly falls down. (Other chapters will teach you to deal with any anger or hostility.) Remember to find the exception to the overgeneralization.

Impossibility Words

Your purpose will be to discover what actual or mental restraints the person has. For example, there can be a variety of meanings to the following statements "I *can't* sign the order," "I *couldn't* do that," or "We *shouldn't* make a decision just yet." While all of these are possibly true, you want to find out why. The words actually put a limit on your clients' thinking which may not be useful to you or to them. Discovering the reason behind the statement allows you to uncover the real situation that must be dealt with.

"I can't sign the order" might mean that the person doesn't have the authority or that something else is in the way. Either way, it is important information for you to know.

"I couldn't do that." Why not? What would happen if you did? Again, by questioning, you get valuable information.

"We shouldn't make a decision just yet" may be indicating a desire to procrastinate or some hidden mental rule which says, "never make an impulsive decision." By asking, "Why not?" you obtain information that you can potentially work with.

In conclusion, almost anything a person says can be significant to you. You merely need to ask to clarify. When you ask and then listen carefully, people tell you almost everything you need to know to persuade them. Unlike the traditional sales approach of "challenging" the prospect or client, you have learned to accept what the client says as wholly or partly true for the moment and then to work with it or around it. This is ethical selling. This approach will allow you to "win friends and influence people."

You also learned how words mean different things to different people and how it is sometimes imperative to use the same definition they are using. Other situations call for you to appreciate that the client may have certain mental limitations because of the particular words or phrases being used. Your primary concern, again, is to work through or around those limitations so that you both have a satisfactory outcome.

While we have been using sales situations as the primary examples, you undoubtedly appreciate that the same things apply to almost all other areas of your life. Once you begin to pay attention to the meanings behind the words, you begin to increase your effectiveness as a communicator. Throughout the book we will return to getting the meaning hidden behind the words.

The next chapter will provide some basic verbal skills to assist you in gathering information. These are fundamental skills that will help you more easily gather all of the information discussed thus far.

6

Conversational Skills

The greatest attribute of a great conversationalist is to be a great listener. If you want people to like you, merely pay attention to what they have to say rather than what you have to say. Listening is more than merely hearing. It involves making appropriate responses, verifying your understanding, and using conversational skills to assist the process.

All of the things you've learned thus far require that you be able to effectively gather information. For the most part, you will do this verbally—and the most effective way to do it is in a conversational manner. These skills are essential to effective presentations.

The techniques described in this chapter are found in the tool kit of virtually every successful salesperson. The chapter contains verbal skills used in virtually every sales and communication course on the market. Although the courses use varying terminology, we find that the important skills are virtually identical from course to course. These skills provide the foundation for all conversations.

Most experts mention two broad skills as important to selling: listening and speaking. Both are equally important to the overall process. Practicing the verbal skills enables you to become more effective at presenting your sales story.

Listening Versus Hearing

Listening is much more than merely hearing. Your ear hears. Your brain listens. At a social gathering you may hear several conversations going on around you, but you participate in only one. *Listening* attaches meaning to what you believe to be important to your purposes. During the conversation, you must listen carefully and respond effectively so that you can get closer to your goal. Listening is about the most important space in the world...the distance between the eardrum and the brain.

Selective Listening

Selective listening is like panning for the gold in your prospect's or client's words. It means you pay attention to all that is expressed verbally as well as nonverbally, but you select only what is relevant for your response in accordance with your purposes. Likewise, as previously discussed, you are gathering information. Often the specific things that will help you understand this person are hidden within the broader context of the conversation. You should devote attention to discovering these hidden meanings.

Responsive Listening

Responsive listening means that you acknowledge what your prospect or client says without making value judgments. Making noncommittal statements such as "Uh-huh," "I see," and "Tell me more" and asking additional questions about what is being said indicate that you are listening responsively. This is also called client-centered listening. Again, *the trick to being a great conversationalist is to be a great listener.*

There's More to It than Just Talk

Body language is also very important. What are the facial expressions telling you? Is your prospect or client showing excitement, surprise, or displeasure? Is the person slouching or sitting attentively? Is the eye contact wandering or focused on you? All these signals help to convey your prospect's or client's attitude toward you. As in everything, the tone of the voice can give you information. Does it indicate interest, boredom, or resistance? You must attend to more than the words in the message.

As discussed in the previous chapter, you should challenge your own assumptions. While a particular physical posture of a prospect *might* have significance, it could also be meaningless. The best idea is to check it out. Unfortunately, other people will not have the same understanding that you now have. They probably have not learned the importance of challenging assumptions. They will probably do quite a bit of mind reading based upon how they perceive you. Fortunately, you can determine what image you show the world.

What are your facial expressions and body language telling people about you? Do you look interested?...bored?...angry?...enthusiastic? Your body language and tone of voice must show enthusiasm and belief in yourself and your value because you, too, are continually broadcasting unconscious messages.

You should probably ask a few of your friends to do you a favor by commenting on how others might typecast you. Do you like the image you present to the world? Anything they say is useful information, because you can make modifications to your body language to create in other people the automatic response you want.

Barriers to Effective Listening

These barriers are common, so the warnings below are extremely important. If you don't pay proper attention to them, you could ruin any chances you have for success. Given conscious attention, these barriers are easy to avoid or you can at least minimize their effects.

Presuming

Don't presume you know what a person will say: listen to the person. Whenever you presume, you significantly decrease your probability of success. The best technique of all is to listen without making judgments.

Distractions

Think about what you're hearing, and control the environmental distractions as much as possible. Look at the person. Smile when they smile. Say "uh-huh" once in a while. Use their name often; that will keep their attention on you, and people usually positively respond to their name.

Rushing

Avoid rushing or pushing your client. Rushing someone is almost a sure road to failure. It can make a sales pro seem desperate, and nobody wants to deal with a desperate sales pro. Take the time to listen to the person. Utilize the rapport skills that will be presented.

Interrupting

Interrupting is even worse than rushing. The more you listen, the better they will like you. If possible, try to avoid interrupting their speech patterns. (There are some people who are so boring that if you don't change the subject they will drive you crazy, or so talkative that they totally dominate the discussion. The closed-ended question technique that will be discussed below will help you with such people because it is simply a matter of directing the conversation to obtain the results you want.)

Inattention—Real or Imagined

You have a purpose in mind—allowing the person to feel comfortable with you; you won't achieve your purpose unless you pay attention to them. We've all probably had the experience of watching a person go into never-never land while we are talking to them. Their eyes seem to get glassy, and you know they are mentally somewhere else. Sometimes they are just thinking. But just as you dislike it when a person isn't listening to you, other people will dislike it when you aren't listening to them.

To keep your attention on them it may help to focus on some of the verbal patterns they are using. You will, at least, continue to look interested. When the other person starts to drift use their name, and they'll quickly refocus their attention on what you have to say. If they drift too often, change your style or suggest another meeting after you have verified that everything is okay.

Planning What to Say Next

Wait until the other person finishes speaking before you formulate your answers. Hear the person out first so that you get the full message. Then you can figure out how you want to respond.

Tools for Effective Listening

In addition to listening you must also employ a few other highly effective tools. Once again, the following techniques are basic to communication. Practicing them one at a time, and then in combination, will make you more persuasive and powerful—allowing you to achieve your ends more often.

Questioning Techniques

You may already be familiar with the techniques of open and closed probes. If so, this short section will enable you to review the way these skills are used in various conversations.

The goal of probing is to uncover information and/or direct the conversation.

Open-Ended Probes.   A question or statement that encourages the person to speak freely about a topic of his or her choosing is an open-ended probe. Open probes frequently use the following key words: *what, how,* and *why*. Phrases such as *tell me more, what else?, uh-huh,* etc., also encourage the person to be even more expansive in his or her explanations.

The more you can get them to talk, the better off you are; the more they share with you, the more they trust and like you. Quickly they begin to feel more and more comfortable with you. You will find this very effective when combined with the rapport skills we will present.

As they feel more comfortable, they begin sharing some of the details about their lives, hopes, likes, aspirations, jobs, etc. Each piece of information actually gets them more and more committed to you because now they must mentally justify giving you so much information about themselves. They may think that you must be a worthwhile, special person—otherwise, they would never have given you the information in the first place. Open probes are effective but only truly effective when combined with listening. Again, *developing your ability to listen is probably one of the best things that you can do.*

Closed-Ended Probes.   A question that steers the person to a specific topic of your choosing and limits the answer to one or two words is a closed-ended probe, for example, "Do you like this idea?" can get you a yes/no answer.

You can use closed-ended questions to verify information, for example, "You really enjoy this idea, right?" Regardless of whether they give you a yes or no response, get them talking by asking "Why?" Their usual response is "Because..." At that point you are again getting information about the things that motivate them.

The rule of thumb is to use open-ended questions as often as possible and get your potential prospect or client talking as much as possible. The more they talk, the better they like you. Asking too many closed-ended questions could make you sound as if you are conducting an interrogation. Closed-ended probes are used when a person is unresponsive to open-ended questions. Some people will seemingly talk forever. Closed-ended probes will allow you to direct the conversation while still allowing them to talk. The only difference is that they are now talking about the topics you wish them to discuss. You also use closed probes to direct the conversation to a new and specific topic — in other words, when you want to change the subject. You have the ability to control the direction of the conversation.

The Skill of Acknowledging

The skill of acknowledging makes the person aware of your attention, understanding, and responsiveness to their concerns. It is a vital part of any conversation and can be accomplished in a variety of ways.

Whenever someone says something to you, he expects that you are listening to what is being said. Something as simple as nodding your head or saying "Uh-huh" could suffice.

Often a person will express a concern which is bothering her. Her concern, because she stated it, has validity. Before you can provide an answer, you must acknowledge the concern. For example, you can respond, "I can understand your concern regarding this idea which is why the following feature should relieve your concern." This response lets your prospect or client know that you've taken her feelings and concerns into consideration.

We have conducted demonstrations over many years and involving thousands of people on the necessity of acknowledging a concern. We will tell the group that we are about to conduct an experiment to demonstrate the effect of not acknowledging someone's concern. We then ask for a volunteer to give us any concern that he or she may have. It could be about the weather, politics, a toothache, or anything relevant to that person. When the concern is expressed, we provide a solution to the problem without acknowledging that we heard the person. Two or three sentences later we'll stop the experiment and poll the group. Usually the volunteer as well as 50 percent of the group will feel that we were insulting, uncaring, and unconcerned about his or her feelings. The group reacts this way even though they know what we are going to do ahead of time! Most people are surprised at the overall reaction and further surprised when they realize that the concern was actually addressed, though not using the specific skill of acknowledging. This is an intuitive, unconscious, automatic response which you are now aware of.

Your best intentions in the world are useless if the person you are talking with has his or her feathers ruffled. Acknowledging is a skill worth practicing and using regularly.

There are many ways to acknowledge a concern. One method which has been popularized in various sales courses is the Feel-Felt-Found method. It works like this: "I understand how you *feel* (indicating understanding and/or empathy); other people *felt* that way (indicating that the concern is reasonable and that other people's initial concern, by definition of the past tense, has been resolved); but they *found* that _____ (indicating that a particular feature, benefit, or advantage provided the solution to the concern).

This is an effective method which, it should be explained, includes alternative responses. "I can see what you're concerned about, other people had indicated something similar, and when they saw that _____" or "I hear what you're saying. Other people expressed a similar concern and were pleased to hear that _____." (The reasons will be made clearer.)

The Skill of Linking

Have you ever been involved in a conversation in which it took you a few moments to figure out what the other person was talking about? If you are like most people, you have experienced such situations. For whatever reason, you did not make the transition to the next phase of the conversation. For a moment you were lost and slightly confused.

During the sales process you want to make sure that the client is with you. The skill of linking helps ensure that the other person knows what you are talking about. You do this by making statements such as, "Earlier you mentioned that you wanted to learn more about programming." The client now knows that programming is the current topic of conversation. Bridging allows you to connect an earlier idea with the current subject by easily moving from one topic to another.

The Skill of Building

The skill of building allows you to make a person aware of your respect for his or her ideas by adding value to what the person says. The other person will feel good about you because you are in agreement. For example, "I agree with your comments about that movie. It had excellent photography. In addition, it also had good acting. Don't you agree?" In this example the person is "patted on the head" because you agreed with their comment. Essentially, you repeated or summarized what they said, and, they must agree with you because you agreed with them. Then, you add additional value by making another comment which they will probably agree with. Finally, by asking them for verification, you get them to buy into your added value.

What you are demonstrating is that you are like them. He or she ought to like you because you are so much like them. "I agree that this house has a great kitchen. It also has numerous closets. Correct?"

It's important to remember the sequence. Agree with what they said by repeating it, add additional value, then verify acceptance.

The Skill of Drawing an Analogy

Analogies are a way of saying, "This is the same as..." People are comfortable with what they know. People get a thrill from learning something new and different. Yet many people are afraid of making a mistake in front of others because they believe they would look or sound stupid and uninformed. So analogies provide a way to make the new fit in by relating it to the familiar.

Sometimes a conversation may get bogged down because a prospect may have trouble understanding exactly how something, such as your product, service, or whatever you happen to be talking about works. This is particularly true if they are not knowledgeable about your product or service. When this situation arises, it is helpful to have an alternative explanation that explains what you just said in a different way. When you draw an analogy, you put your comments in a series of examples that the other person can understand.

For example, imagine that you are trying to explain a clogged fuel filter problem in your car to someone who barely knows where the gas tank is but does know how to cook. "You mentioned before that you like to cook. You know how sometimes bits of food get stuck in the baster and clog it? Well, that's basically what happens when you have a clogged fuel line—a piece of dirt prevents the gas from getting through."

The idea is to make people feel good about learning something new using references that they already know. They feel good about themselves, they feel good about you. You both win.

If the nature of your product or service is unusual or difficult for many people to comprehend, spend some time thinking about how you can explain it to someone else using relatively simple analogies. You should have five or six different ways of explaining the same thing, each using a different example. Be wary of making it so simple that you insult the other person's intelligence. Avoid sounding sarcastic or condescending—that would be a sure way to lose a potential sale.

So far, everything that has been said has been intended to make you a better conversationalist. The ability to listen is very important. The ability to speak intelligently is almost as important.

Just One More Thing to Becoming a Great Conversationalist

A good conversationalist must also actually have something to say. It isn't all listening and adding value. It is helpful to have a working knowledge of local, national, and international events. Watch the news often and skim all sections of a magazine like Time *or* U.S. News & World Report *or a good daily newspaper, because they cover a range of topics—everything from art and music to politics, etc. Although you may not be interested in some or most of these topics, your prospect or client may be. Having a conversational knowledge of the topics of the day is simply another tool of managing the sales story in an effective way.*

PART 3

Sales

Top salespeople are among the highest paid professionals in the world, and rightly so. Manufactured products, sitting in a warehouse, are basically worthless until they are sold. Each company in the world provides a product or service that must be "sold" to someone else. If there are enough sales, the company prospers (assuming that the product is good). If sales fall too sharply, the company may fail.

It is common to find salespeople in an organization being paid more than the company president. In sales, your income is potentially unlimited — it is based solely on your ability to produce. There are no other professions that I can think of where this is generally true.

There is a price to pay for this level of success. Selling is a profession which requires a tremendous amount of dedication and desire to be great. In a sense, it is like sports. Trying to be good isn't good enough. Selling requires practice and judgment regarding which ideas are worth implementing.

We both know that when you really want something there is nothing in the world that can stop you. Nothing. However, you may have to do things that other people would find too difficult. That doesn't make it easy to reach your goal, it makes it possible to do so.

Client satisfaction is the name of the game. The best salespeople realize this and are constantly searching for ways to become even better; to more completely satisfy their clients' needs; to more fully penetrate the account. They uncover needs that the average salesperson never even imagines, resulting in a corresponding increase in their compensation.

However, discovering how your products and services can meet a client's needs is only one side of the coin. The other side is effectively con-

vincing that person that you are the one to deal with. Making effective presentations is the subject of this section.

A professional regularly evaluates his or her performance. Here are a few questions to assist in that process. You should ask yourself why? *or* why not? *after answering each of them.*

1. *Did the transaction represent quality?*
2. *Did I increase the client's trust in myself and in my firm?*
3. *Did I earn the client's respect?*
4. *Did I solve a problem or fulfill a need for this person?*
5. *Did I act in a professional manner?*
6. *If our roles were reversed, would I have been satisfied with the transaction?*

Additionally, the highest-level professionals are always seeking to improve. They always ask the questions:

What specifically did I do right?

What specifically did I do wrong?

What could I do even better next time?

What did I learn?

7

What's Your Story?—Preparing for an Effective Presentation

Getting to yes is the goal of selling. That is, your sales effort is designed to bring the client to say, "Yes, I want your service, and where do I sign."

How do you make a sales presentation that will have the desired effect? As you might expect, there are some rules. These rules work in all situations because they take into account how human nature works.

It's fascinating, the absolutely best salespeople seem to tell effective sales stories that are made up on the spot from materials provided by the client. However, in reality, these stories are anything but impromptu. These salespeople employ a precise methodology, although sometimes unconsciously. There are many skills that must be learned before such sales magic can occur.

Questioning skills are used to get the ingredients of the story, and these ingredients are then blended into a story that the client wants to hear. That is, you must tell a very good story from the client's point of view.

Related instances of storytelling include a commercial that tells a story, a television show or a movie story, and the cross look a parent may direct at a child. Similarly, the sales professional tells a story whose message is "Why this offering is good for you."

So, What's Your Story?

You've probably heard prospects or clients say, "So, what's your story?" It is not coincidental that in a sales situation a client would use such a phrase. As you now realize, the everyday words people use are very useful indicators of how they think. In this case, the client expressed an expectation regarding your presentation. Our society is story-oriented. We thrive on it. Unconsciously, we demand it. The best presentations fulfill these unconscious expectations.

Preliminary Information Needed

Before you can put together a good story, there are a few preliminary things which must occur. First and foremost, you *must* identify the client's needs. The client's needs must come first. Start with, "How can I help you?" and continue with the key questions previously discussed. Armed with this vitally important information, you will then be able to make a persuasive presentation. Of course, this assumes that your product line can fulfill the need.

The process you are about to learn is usually accomplished while you are getting your initial data. That is, as you are speaking to the client, the answers you are given will fit into one or more of the categories we will discuss.

Start with the Happy Ending

A good story, of course, has a beginning, a middle, and an end. So does a good sales presentation, although it is called the opening, the presentation, and the close. Each will be discussed separately.

In selling we often find it is better to start with the ending of the story. That means we define the client's version of a happy ending as our starting place. Then, other elements easily fall into place.

You begin with the ending the client wants, learn about the situation the client is in, and close the sale — the happy ending for you and the client.

The questions, "What do you want in a _____?" and "What would _____ do for you?" usually define the client's happy ending. When you keep these two answers in mind, the sales presentation is merely an explanation of how the happy ending is achieved.

It's important to realize that you will rarely get all of the information on the first pass. Selling is like a dance in which there is a lot of give and take. You ask questions and get initial information. This information is incorporated into the presentation. The client responds to certain parts of the presentation better than to others. You modify your presentation accordingly.

The happy ending must have four important conditions to be "realistic," as well as to allow you and the client to "win" and for the transaction to be "worth it" to you both. They are:

- The desired results must be specifically identified in the story.
- The story must fulfill the client's rules for proof.
- The happy ending must truly be happy.
- The happy ending must be more than a dream.

The Desired Results Must Be Specifically Identified in the Story

Providing the client with a specific goal to be achieved allows the client's mind to focus on the positive end result that he or she previously identified. Once these goals are identified, they become the target at which your presentation is aimed. The features, advantages, and benefits that you present will be those most relevant to the client's objectives. You'll also find that many unnecessary objections and concerns just seem to disappear when the client's primary or overall goals are the focus of the presentation.

The Story Must Fulfill the Client's Rules for Proof

Each person has a way of measuring the outcome of a buying decision. Some people will take your word for it that they got a good deal; they are rare, but you may encounter them occasionally. Others will want to let a little time go by before they become convinced that your offering hasn't any flaws. Still others will want the opinion of someone they trust. Possibly most convincing of all, for most people, is a demonstration. One of your primary responsibilities is to be able to to prove your offering works for the client according to the client's rules of proof.

You will need to discover the client's rules. The simplest way to do this is to ask: "How will you know for sure that this is the right thing for you?" or "How will you know you made the right decision?"

Do not settle for vague or abstract answers to this question. You need specifics. Ultimately, your reputation and your company's reputation is on the line. If the client has a criterion for proof that is unreasonable, then you want to know that up front; otherwise, the relationship is doomed to failure. It is easy to offset an unreasonable expectation if it is discovered early in your discussions. It is much more difficult to deal with it after the sale, because the client has been holding on to that expectation and probably thinks that it is reasonable. This may have even been a reason that he or she wanted to buy your product in the first place.

While it is not always possible to uncover such expectations, you can at least try.

The Happy Ending Must Truly Be Happy

What you are offering should produce no negative side effects from your client's point of view. There are at least two levels of importance to this notion. The outcome the client will want usually takes the form of less cost, less time, less hassle, or, conversely, more convenience, more gains for less effort, and so on. Beyond the features that come with the outcome, there is also an outcome to the outcome, which can also be called an ulterior motive. That is, if your service or product works as well as it should, you have achieved the first outcome. The outcome of that outcome is that the client will gain something else. She may be satisfied personally, her reputation may be improved, she may get a promotion, her boss may be very pleased, or some other result of the result will emerge from the success of your offering. This information is often obtained as a result of the question "And what would having _____ do for you?"

Here is an unfortunate situation that happened to a friend of ours. John needed to do word processing. He was a neophyte to computers and knew absolutely no technical terminology. At a large retail store he approached a salesman (unfortunately, also a rookie) and indicated that he wanted something which was easy and convenient to use so he could do word processing. He wanted something more than a typewriter. John was sold a very nice portable computer. He was rather pleased with his purchase until, while at work some weeks later, he discovered that the computer could not run any of the word processing or spreadsheet software used by his company. It was too late to return the computer. John was out of luck and very displeased with himself, the computer, the store, the manufacturer, and especially, the salesman.

If the salesman had asked, "And what would having this do for you," he would have discovered that John wanted to run the other types of programs used at his office. The well-meaning salesman could have then sold John a computer more appropriate to his needs. All he needed to do was ask.

The Happy Ending Must Be More Than a Dream

On occasion, clients will attempt to solve problems that are beyond their ability or authority to solve. Whether the client is in a family business or corporation, he or she must have the authority and budget to reach an outcome that is satisfying to you both. If the client must get approvals from someone else, you may be talking to the wrong person. These approvals can take many forms. Sometimes a certified public accountant, banker, attorney, spouse, or other trusted adviser must be consulted. If so, you want to know this so that you can include the other person and thereby maximize your probability of success.

Also, any promises you make must be within your control to deliver. We know of many unfortunate situations where the salesperson promised a delivery date that the manufacturing division could not meet. Regardless of the reason for the failure, the client is disappointed.

Real—Win—Worth

The four conditions just discussed can be easily checked with the real—win—worth questions.

Is This Sales Situation "for Real"?

There are times when client expectations are out of line with reality. For instance, "This product will solve all my problems and answer the questions of life, the universe, and everything," or "This economy model car will let me go drag racing."

There are other times when the salesperson's idea of what should happen is out of line with reality, like when promises are made that the company cannot or will not keep. These are the situations that are often referred to as someone "blowing smoke." Sales professionals are very aware of their company's ability to deliver. This includes operational, manufacturing, and delivery issues. They realize that it is easier to be careful than

*to go back on their word. Most clients will be quite reasonable if you ne-
gotiate with them rather than promising them the moon.*

Is This a "Win-Win" Situation for
You and Your Client?

If your client feels you are a ripoff artist before or after the sale and has
buyer's remorse, you both lose. If you feel you must fudge your story or
be manipulative, you are probably not in a win-win situation. In this instance it is useful to know what the client will use as "proof."

Is This Effort "Worth It" in Terms of
Payoff for You Both?

If you must make unreasonable concessions or put up with unreasonable behavior or lose money on the sale, it is probably not worth it to
you. Nor is it worth it to your client if your representations to the client
are not accurate or if the sale backfires in some way.

Here again are the four conditions, repeated as questions:

- Are the desired results specifically identified?
- Are the client's rules for proof fulfilled?
- Do the results produce a good outcome?
- Is the situation within the client's control?

Also, remember to ask the real—win—worth questions, which will
help you check for the above conditions:

- Is this sales situation "for real"?
- Is this a "win-win" situation for you and your client?
- Is this effort "worth it" in terms of payoff for you both?

*If the answers to these questions are not all positive, you may have a
problem, such as a product or service you don't believe in. It is also possible that you have mixed motives, lack of know-how, or even an impossible situation. In any case, whatever the specifics of your situation, you
are well advised to examine things very closely until you can find out how
to get positive answers to all of these issues. Otherwise, your setup has the
seeds of disappointment built into it.*

Traditional Themes

People are motivated by common human needs, which many experts have defined in different ways. But in general, people are motivated toward things they like and away from things they don't like. Since everyone has different life experiences, people are unique in how they think about what they want.

Yet there are common themes and motives shared by all that cut across the uniqueness of individuals. The back covers of paperback novels provide samples such as power, greed, romance, rivalry, money, and many more. So, too, in sales. In a sales context a common observation about human nature shows one typical desire of people, i.e., wanting more results for less effort. The home appliance industry has made a great deal of profit on this idea with labor-saving devices.

The Client Is the Hero of the Story

It is his story, not yours. And if you ask very carefully, he will let you know how to tell him a winning story that he will like. The client/hero is also the good guy, and the client is always right—at least from his perspective. Understanding is relative to the individual. We caution you against judging the perspective of others. Act on the assumption of different strokes for different folks. You may wish to expand his understanding, but even when you do, allow your presentation to remain his story.

Clients have various ways of defining how they get to be the hero of the story. These examples may also touch upon your idea of how to be the star of your situation. "The hero (client's name) saves the day," or "...comes through again," or "...meets his budget," or "...gains a great reputation," and so on. This is an aspect of the outcome of the outcome.

The Basic Function of the Story

The prime issue is to tell a story that will change a mind. There is also development in the story. In sales, you and the client both learn a great deal about each other. You change how you go about telling your story as you get reactions from the client to your moves. You adjust your thinking accordingly. You will learn how she decides and her criteria for knowing a good thing when she sees it...such as your product or service.

You Already Tell Good Stories

You may think you have no skill along these lines. Actually, you have a great deal of skill in this area. For instance, have you told a friend or family member about how you went shopping for a new car? That story may have only taken a minute or two or maybe much longer. Consider the story elements that have been mentioned here. Most if not all of them were present. The conclusion is obvious: it seems you know how to tell a story. Arranging the ingredients in storytelling is the way to a more convincing story which will achieve a more definitive and desired response.

Offering the Client a Better Way

Sales represents one of the highest callings: the professional has the ability to so thoroughly entrance a person that the salesperson can bring about a mutually beneficial result, one that neither of you could have had without the other. The client gets something better than before (by some measure); the sales pro gets something better than before (by some measure). For the client it might be speed, service, or low cost. For the sales pro it might be a bonus, recognition, or the achievement of a personal goal.

Not many people can claim to have as their daily agenda the desire to make something better for someone else. It is because you offer to make things better for your prospect that she will become your client. You must be able to tell her how much good you can do for her. That calls for a magical ability to tell the client a really good story that convinces her to accept your offer. If you are convincing, she will buy.

8

To Script or Not to Script— That Is the Question

Over the years I've been at the receiving end of more than a few horrendous canned presentations. I can agree with many salespeople that certain types of scripts are a waste of time. A totally memorized presentation, repeated verbatim, over and over is probably a waste of your talents. It is fine for rookies, because they often initially need a crutch. However, once they've practiced it a few times, they should be making adaptations based on how clients respond.

The ultimate demonstration of how not to use a script was demonstrated in an old TV show called "Taxie." Jim read a script so exactly that his presentation went something like this: "Hello, Mr. or Mrs. Name of Person here. I am happy to be here. My name is give Your Name, but you can call me Nickname. What a lovely home you have. May I come in?" While ludicrous, it's not too far from the performance of some poor salespeople who seem to be trying to read their entire script in one breath. That is the negative side of scripting.

While we do not believe in a word-for-word script, we do think you should create an extensive outline which carefully and precisely chooses the words most able to accomplish your task.

The extensive, rehearsed outline is designed to present concepts in the most opportune manner possible. It should allow time for client feedback. This ensures that the client is following the presentation, and gives you the opportunity to make any adaptations.

It should be designed to elicit a yes response to whatever you are proposing. Through the use of periodic questions within the presentation, you determine the client's response to your suggestions. The questions ensure that the client's concerns are addressed at the appropriate time and that you stay on track.

Scripts Don't Have to Sound Canned

Actors seem to be very natural as they play their roles on television or in the movies. Yet they are often scripted to the raising of their eyebrows. Some theater actors give their speeches hundreds of times, and each presentation sounds fresh and wonderful. They demonstrate the other side of the coin — well-rehearsed and thought-out speech can sound elegant.

An Ideal Presentation

Essentially, we are proposing a sales track in which you prepare and practice your presentation in an ideal sequence in order to maximize your effectiveness.

Once the script is prepared, it should be practiced a number of times so that it doesn't sound "canned," i.e., as if it is being read. By practicing the script and identifying and emphasizing key words, benefit statements, etc., you will sound as if you are just talking off the cuff. After the written script is thoroughly reviewed, you'll be able to reduce it to just key words and phrases which will trigger entire sequences of words. Because of this you'll be able to shuffle the presentation sequence as the situation demands, giving you flexibility and adaptability. (This will become very important when personal buying motivations are discussed below.) You'll sound very professional and elegant.

We All Script, Anyway

Some people may think this unnecessary because they can just "wing it." After selling the same product a number of times salespeople begin to habitually use the same words and phrases for all subsequent presentations, that is, the sales routine is habituated. In reality, such salespeople have unconsciously written a script, and the presentation is about 90 percent the same from one client to the next.

This is how it works: the typical salesperson makes a presentation for the first time and realizes that certain parts of the presentation work well and others parts don't. Basically, the presentation is rough. Minor modifications are made with the next client and so on until a dozen or so presentations have been made. Eventually, the salesperson is saying the same thing to each person. It may have taken 10 to 50 presentations before she can give it smoothly and feel confident and comfortable that all the bases have been covered. Once that happens, the closing ratio (the number of sales versus the number of presentations) increases dramatically.

The key question is during the trial-and-error period how many sales were lost? How much money was lost? How many referrals? Also how many bad habits, poor phraseology, and ineffective comments slipped in during this start-up phase? These negatives will tend to remain in all future presentations because they are now habitual.

A Better Way

Thinking, rehearsing, and scripting ahead of time is much more effective and efficient. The start-up time required to have a good sales story is significantly reduced. Instead of making major refinements after the fact, you've made the major refinements before the fact.

You will fine-tune your presentation as you go along. Eventually, after multiple presentations, you'll have a much better presentation because the built-in errors have been kept to an absolute minimum. You will have a presentation that really works for you, and you will have made numerous additional sales in the meantime. You will have gotten to that "natural" spot much earlier because you planned ahead.

If you were an attorney about to defend your brief before the Supreme Court, you would practice. If you were an executive about to make a speech, you would practice. If you were an actor in a major motion picture, you would practice and practice till you could say your lines in your sleep. If you were the President of the United States about to give the State of the Union address, you would certainly practice.

You are a professional who relies on your words and delivery to make your living. Your livelihood depends on your ability to effectively motivate and persuade. How professional do you want to be?

Professionals rehearse and practice their art. That's what makes them professionals. It's your choice. You can be the best you possibly can be, consistently and on demand, or you can be mediocre. A good way to practice is to purchase a tape recorder and then listen to yourself. Try to get assistance from one or two friends. They'll make note of speech patterns that you may not even be aware of. Additionally, they'll serve as a live person you can talk to.

Point of View

The sales presentation can be regarded as a dialogue between the salesperson and the client. We'll examine the presentation from the salesperson's viewpoint first.

The Salesperson's Point of View

It is traditionally taught that sales presentations should be prepared using an outline which addresses the important aspects of your product or service. If you are able to respond to these questions, you are considered adequately prepared to make the sale. The questions are good. Let us briefly review the most important ones.

- *Who is my audience?* Who am I preparing my presentation for?
- *What is the need?* From previous conversations this person has indicated a need or want that I can fulfill. What is it?
- *What is the solution?* Which product or service will best meet the client's need?
- *What are the benefits?* How is the client going to benefit? Which are the most important benefits? Which will be most meaningful? How do I best express the benefits?
- *What is the evidence for my claims?* What proof do I have? (Product performance reports, testimonials, etc.)
- *What are the concerns?* What concerns and/or objections will the cli-

ent probably or potentially raise? How do I overcome these concerns?

Overcoming client concerns or resistance *is a common phrase in most sales training material. Be aware that it implies a type of confrontation where you win the point. I suggest that you mentally substitute the word* respond *for* overcome. *If you do so, it will create a more positive, unconscious response from you when a client brings up a question or concern.*

- Summarize the features, benefits, and advantages. Review the strongest elements of your presentation.
- Ask for the order. Apply one of the closing techniques available.

This approach *does work.* It is logically sequenced and will certainly help someone prepare a pretty good presentation. However, it does need a bit of refinement in that it really does not take the psychology of the client into account.

The Client's Point of View

Now review the same presentation sequence from the point of view of the client. Assume that the salesperson is telephoning the client or prospect. As we said before, there are very few people in the world who are anxiously looking at their telephone and thinking, "I sure hope a salesperson gives me a call to sell me something. Come on, phone, ring." Therefore, realize that the client has been interrupted from something. The salesperson says "Hello" and begins the sales presentation. Meanwhile the client is asking his or her own set of questions:

- What is he talking about?
- Why should I care?
- How is it done?
- What will it do for me?
- How do I know it will work?
- What about...?
- What was that again?
- What do I do now?

Putting Them Together

Here are the two mental monologues merged. When you read them together, keep in mind the need to do things from the client's point of view.

Salesperson	Client
Who is the audience?	What is he talking about?
What is the need?	Why should I care?
What is the solution?	How is it done?
What are the benefits?	What will it do for me?
What is the evidence?	How do I know it will work?
What are the concerns?	What about…?
Summarize	What was that again?
Call for action	What do I do now?

Make sure the point of view you take is the client's and not your own. Use the pronoun you *and the client's name often to keep him connected to the story. It is his needs, and not your product or your ego, that is at issue in the sales process. Remembering this helps you make the client the hero of the story.*

People have a need to win, but make sure it is not at your expense. Nor should you be one-up on the client. You need to position yourself as her equal in helping her meet her needs or there will be other issues that will require extra work on your part. If you feel one-down or one-up as a habit, you might want to talk to someone to break that habit.

Precall Planning

To maximize your effectiveness, it is wise to plan your presentation. The following allows you to mentally structure your talk. It only takes a moment to review, and it will increase your probability of success.

Precall Planning Form

Client:_____

Needs/Objectives:_____

Any specialized needs/objectives:_____

Product to present:_____

Initial need statement to generate interest

1. Restate client's need(s).

2. Probe for accuracy.

3. Refer to general product.

4. Relate general benefit to need(s).

Presentation

1. Refer to specific product.

2. Probe for knowledge and attitude.

3. State specific features and benefits and relate to need(s).

Feature	Benefit
A. _____	_____
B. _____	_____
C. _____	_____
D. _____	_____
E. _____	_____

4. Probe to verify acceptance.

(*Continued*)

Precall Planning Form (*Continued*)

Close

1. Summarize accepted benefits.

2. Request a commitment.

If client has questions or concerns,

1. Probe to get objection as specific as possible.

2. Rephrase objection in question form.

3. Provide appropriate information.

	Possible objections	Appropriate response
A.	_____	_____
B.	_____	_____
C.	_____	_____
D.	_____	_____

Sales Script Format

0pener/Beginning
1. Rationale for call (relate to previously stated need).
2. Benefit statement (don't mention specific product yet; just state the benefit the client will derive from it).
3. Probe for acceptance (permission to proceed). The primary idea is to capture the client's attention and ensure that now is an appropriate time to make the presentation. If for whatever reason the client says no, determine if the situation has changed or if there would be a better time to talk.

Presentation/Middle
1. Give both features and related benefits.
   Just which features and benefits you decide to highlight will, of course, depend on the client to whom you are making the presentation.
2. Break the features and benefits down into small sections, and use frequent checks with the client so you can get feedback—and to prevent selling "past the close."
3. Include some sizzle.
   For a product, this could be a good "story" about an exciting new product or development (if so, optimize the story by telling what the product does and why it is better than others); basically, you will relate what makes the product stand out from the crowd, and why your client will want to brag about his purchase to his friends or associates. Your story could also be the "advantage"; that is, it could illustrate a comparison of why *this* product meets your client's objectives better than *other* products might. Benefits answer your client's question "What does it do for me?" The sizzle could answer your client's question "What am I going to like best about this?" In other words, why buy?
4. Write in at least two standard questions and/or objections, along with your responses, as part of the body of your presentation.

Close/End
1. Ensure that you have responded to any questions or concerns.
2. Summarize why the client is buying, i.e., the benefit statements.
3. Ask for the order (covered in Part 6).
4. Ask for a referral (covered in Part 6).

Before you make the presentation you must also consider both the client's sophistication level and the detail level.

Client's Sophistication Level

If you mentally prepare for two client extremes—very knowledgeable and absolutely ignorant—you will be able to sell almost anyone. With the very knowledgeable client, you may be able to use jargon and present your ideas more succinctly and quickly. A good person to practice with would be a knowledgeable coworker or friend.

You may also deal with clients who know absolutely nothing about any aspect of what you are selling or perhaps know only one aspect. In either case, you must be able to explain your concepts so they can understand. It is important to avoid any jargon with these clients and to explain very simply. Analogies are often helpful here. Good people to practice with are those friends who have absolutely no idea what you do. If you can explain it to them in simplistic terms, you can explain it to a client when your explanation is part of a real presentation.

KISS

Keep It Short and Sweet ensures that your ideas are presented with an appropriate level of detail. Most salespeople oversell. Consequently, more sales have been lost from overselling and providing too much information than from providing too little information. Yet some salespeople insist on trying to tell the client everything they know about the product as well as their philosophies on life. Most clients find such laborious presentations boring; they are certainly inefficient and generally ineffective.

The Three-Level Presentation

As you know, clients are interested in what the product will do for them as individuals. They are interested in the key points as applied to them. Anything extra that you present is both unnecessary and potentially damaging to the sale.

Make your presentations as simple as possible. Present only the bare minimum necessary. If the client needs additional information or explanation, then and only then, do you present more. However, if the client accepts the first level of the presentation, then that is all you provide.

For the sake of example, pretend that you can divide the main body of your presentation into five distinct parts: (1) details on the manufacturing company, (2) competitive edge, (3) technical data, (4) additional uses, and (5) user support services.

Each of the areas should have three levels of potential commentary. Level A represents the headline version in which one to four sentences give the key ideas. This is followed by a question to verify client understanding and acceptance. The client can say yes or no.

The client says yes.   If the client both understands and accepts what you have said, you then continue to part two of the presentation (the competitive edge, in our example) and provide another headline comment. You continue providing the headline versions as long as the client gives you positive responses. If the client is sophisticated and knowledgeable, it should be possible for you to give the entire presentation—regardless of what you are selling—in 1 minute or less.

The client says no.   If, at any headlined segment, the client needs more information, you should be able to provide additional information. You merely explain the headline in additional detail and probe for understanding and/or acceptance. If the client says yes, return to the headline level for the next segment. (It is important to realize that clients can need additional information on one topic but be sophisticated in other areas. By returning to the headline level, you avoid talking down to the client, a practice which usually generates very negative reactions.) If the client still needs additional information and says no to your question probing understanding, then be prepared to give a lot of detailed information. After explaining it in detail, you again go to the headline level.

This approach ensures that you present only the appropriate amount of information to the client. Where additional information is needed, it is given. If none is needed, you have quickly and efficiently made the pertinent points and can go for the close.

Make note of where the client was knowledgeable and where she was not. In future presentations you will then automatically provide the appropriate level of detail. If, for example, the client generally asks technically oriented questions, you can then provide more technical information for that client than you would for others.

After you have made your presentation, whether you are successful or not, you should mentally critique yourself or, better yet, have someone else do it. This ensures that you constantly search for ways to improve yourself.

It is through this constant attention to self-improvement that you can achieve the highest success levels.

Critiquing the Sales Call

Opening Statement

Restated the client's need   ____YES ____NO

Verified accuracy   ____YES ____NO

Referred to a general product   ____YES ____NO

Related a general benefit to the previously stated need   ____YES ____NO

Can do even better by_____

Presentation

Referred to a specific product or service   ____YES ____NO

Probed for client awareness   ____YES ____NO

Stated features and benefits and related them to need   ____YES ____NO

Probed to verify acceptance   ____YES ____NO

Obtained client participation   ____YES ____NO

Can do even better by_____

Close

Summarized benefits accepted by client   ____YES ____NO

Asked for a commitment (closed)   ____YES ____NO

Asked for a referral   ____YES ____NO

Can do even better by_____

9

Dealing with Corporations

This chapter is designed for those readers who now, or may in the future, regularly deal with corporations, governments, or large groups of decision makers. Even if you never anticipate dealing with such large entities, the information presented below should be useful to you when you work with individuals. You never know when you may get lucky and make more money in one corporate sale than you could make in 2 years of retail sales. When you are actively prospecting, you never know what may come your way.

If you are trying to make presentations to the corporate market, you have to be even more sophisticated than if you were presenting to the retail client. The very large corporations receive many competitive presentations. Sometimes the "difference that makes the difference" is how much mental homework you do on the factors that will influence the decision.

What to Elicit about a Company

When dealing with some organizations you may need to do preliminary work before they consider you a qualified vendor. Many companies use a committee approach to decision making. The committee may include some people who have vested interests in competing products. There's an old joke that says, "A camel is a horse, designed by a committee. While an elephant is a mouse built to government specifications."

Initial Checklist

Here is an initial list of questions that you can use when approaching the corporation. The questions are not all-inclusive, but they will give you a few ideas that you can use. This information will be helpful when you begin preparing your presentation.

1. What is the organizational structure (the total cast on the organization chart)?
   - Who is your contact?
   - What is his or her function?
   - Who does he or she report to?
   - Who must be convinced?
   - Who is the buyer (the decision maker)?
   - What is the budget cycle?
   - What are their buzzwords?

2. Who is your product or service designed for?
   - What is their function (sales, management, clerical staff, etc.)?
   - What is their background (experience, age, education)?
   - How will they use it?

3. What difference(s) do they want us to make?
   - Improving results (regarding productivity or efficiency)?
   - Meeting their needs?
   - Improving the bottom line?

4. How do they do things now?
   - General structure and setup?
   - What do they use now?
   - How do they like what they have now?
   - What do they like about the current programs?
   - What can be improved (from their point of view)?
   - What do they lack or need?
   - How, specifically, will you be able to help?

5. Do they have a preference for how to make the changes they want?
   - Place
   - Time
   - Customized plan — What are previous plans that have been acceptable to them?
   - Transition period

New technologies, equipment, and procedures require varying times to implement. People in general are hesitant about changing. Realize that many people will initially resist the new in favor of leaving things the way they are.

6. How will your performance be measured?
   - Is there a particular format required for the proposal?
   - How will they know they are satisfied?

These questions should assist you in obtaining the initial information that will help to differentiate you from all of your competitors. If possible, read as much information about the company, its philosophy, its history, and its product line as possible. A quick visit to most libraries or brokerage firms will yield a good deal of information. Ask to see either the Standard & Poor's or Moody's manuals. These contain a wealth of information. Additionally, the public relations departments of most companies will be pleased to send you a press kit or an annual report.

Depending upon your product line, the above may seem like overkill. From experience we can only suggest that the more you know about the company the better off you are. This is especially true when you are dealing with big-ticket items or the upper management levels.

Politics

Assume that you have done all the homework that you need to present the features, benefits, and advantages of your product. You know that your product or service can be used by the corporation.

While good looks and logic *may* carry the day, there are often hidden agendas (internal political issues) that may affect the final outcome. The checklist presented below may help you get a sale which otherwise would be lost.

Twenty Areas to Consider When Preparing a Sales Presentation to a Corporation or Your Own Company

This checklist can be used by someone making a proposal to his or her own company as well as by a salesperson targeting a corporation. Think of it as a way to control or influence as many variables as possible. Sometimes the answers will make you realize that you have to do some politicking or information gathering yourself. Occasionally you will not be able to find an answer, or perhaps, the question may not be pertinent to your situation. The checklist will also help you anticipate any objections or roadblocks to the implementation of your idea. Read it carefully. You'll probably find yourself referring to it often.

There is a bit of intentional redundancy in the questions. This ensures that key factors are considered in various contexts.

1. Key objectives
   - What is the main difference my efforts will make? In other words, what am I trying to do?
   - What is my objective?
   - What are the main obstacles and problems to reaching my objectives?
   - *How will the company be better as a result of my idea?*
   - Who, besides me, knows it?
   - What will be the results to me, to the department, to the corporation?
   - What changes will occur as a result of this proposal?

2. Issues and momentum
   - What are the major issues and needs of the decision makers or clients who I must influence?
   - *What pressures do they have from internal or external sources?*
   - How can they be converted from indifference or resistance to support for the issues that advance my cause?

3. Key issue(s) — Rally round the flag
   - Which issue (assuming there are multiple issues) will serve best as the keystone of my program in generating support and success?
   - Which issue will likely have a common denominator that will appeal to most or all of those affected by it?
   - Will the key issues vary in context, in type, or in emphasis during the process?
   - Will they vary among different clients or various associates of clients?

4. Potential allies
   - Who can I count on as allies, and who will assist me?
   - Who are natural allies, and who must be cultivated?
   - Where will individual payoffs be effected positively or negatively by this proposal?
   - Why would they support it?

5. Factors affecting support
   - Will I be able to get the necessary resources and support?
   - How will these clients react under stress or adverse conditions?
   - What could go wrong?

6. Potential opposition
   - Who or what will be my primary opposition and source of resistance?
   - What is the best way to overcome the problem or issue?
   - How do they view the incentives and payoffs represented by this proposal?
   - Who has the most and least to lose if my proposal is accepted? That is, what are the political risks to the participants involved and affected?
   - What are competitive products and services? What are their strengths and weaknesses? Am I competitive?

7. Presentation mode
   - What are the best ways to package and communicate the primary issue to change the minds of the resisters?
   - How can I combine my presentation with my own career advancement (commissions) to best advantage?

8. Key objective
   - Can I write my objective in the form of a newspaper headline? (If you can't say it briefly, you will not easily get your message across.)

9. Timing
   - What is the best timing and method(s) to use to talk to and persuade all those involved and affected by the proposal(s). (*Suggestion:* Gain a consensus on "needs" that will be addressed and then a consensus on optional solutions that are available.)

10. My personal assumptions and reactions
    - Do I take it for granted that there will be a pro, a con, and a neutral reaction to any idea proposed?
    - Have I included my own reactions as a function of how people perceive my interests versus their interests?
    - How will I react if they don't see it my way?

11. How-to issues
    ▪ Do I know the how-to tactics of selling and persuasion to change con and neutral minds to pro?
    ▪ Do I know how to keep pro minds from changing to con or neutral as events evolve?
    ▪ If I don't know, how can I get someone to do it for me or learn how to do it myself?
    ▪ If things don't go my way, what would be the best reaction?
    ▪ How might I salvage all or some of the situation?

12. Hidden agendas
    ▪ Do I know how to get past hidden agendas and secret concerns of those with competing ideas and agendas?
    ▪ Do I know or can I find out for sure who is pro, con, or neutral?

13. How to determine payoffs
    ▪ Should I use group meetings or individual interviews to elicit payoff perceptions and to sell my views among the pro, con, and neutral individuals?

14. Gaining support
    ▪ Whose support in the hierarchy will change others' minds (whether through coercion, example, encroachment, fiat, or whatever)?
    ▪ How do I get that support?
    ▪ Why should they support me?

15. Events which may affect my outcome
    ▪ What events must be controlled, anticipated, and used (e.g., timing, resources, conflicts, human, calendar, environmental, financial, etc.) that will affect support or resistance in the user audience?
    ▪ What is the budget cycle?
    ▪ Is there anything special happening which could help or hurt me?

16. The decision makers
    ▪ At what level will the consensus or the decision be made?
    ▪ Who are the people at that level?
    ▪ How can I reach them and influence their decision and thinking?
    ▪ Can I meet them under different circumstances? Do they attend specific social events? What are their hobbies?

17. Reality check
    - Am I being naively idealistic in thinking that others ought to want the product because I'm convinced that it's a good idea?

18. Working with the politics?
    - Do I see the problem of eliciting support as analogous to a political campaign where I shepherd all events toward a decisive positive vote for my project?

19. How to be viewed most advantageously
    - What role is best for me to use as a thinking tool? (External consultant? Adviser? Expert? Liaison? Facilitator? Organizer? Communicator? Broker?)

20. Additional payoffs
    - Do I know what different people consider as payoffs even if I wouldn't think of those things as payoffs? (Who is motivated by Power, Affiliation, Achievement, etc.?)

PART 4

The Powerful Unconscious Processes

What is that certain "chemistry" that exists between some people and not others? What are its elements? Can chemistry be replicated at will? The answers to these questions are explored here.

There are many fine books which provide some of the elements that make up an initial favorable impression. It has been suggested that an initial impression—good or bad—is made within 3 seconds. Whether or not this is fair is immaterial. How we look, talk, and act contributes to the feeling in another person that "this person is like me" or "...not like me." In fact, these unconscious processes constitute between 75 to 90 percent of all decisions.

Fortunately, we can "package" ourselves to create the image we want to initially project. This package provides the first opportunity we have to influence others unconsciously. The next opportunity to positively influence a person occurs when we begin communicating.

Communication occurs on both the conscious and the unconscious levels. How to develop, enhance, and maintain rapport on the unconscious level is the subject of the next few pages. Unconscious rapport is initially dependent upon how you "pace" the other person. To pace another person means to agree with or to align yourself mentally with him or her. It is being or becoming like other people so that you get their attention and friendship.

There are many ways you can pace another person and thereby establish rapport. The methods presented in this part fall into three basic categories:

Physical

Mental

Emotional

"People like those who are most like themselves," literally and figuratively. As social beings we tend to associate with those people to whom we can most easily and comfortably relate. We respond to people on three primary levels: physical, mental, and emotional. Those to whom we can relate on multiple levels often become friends. If you want someone to form a favorable impression of you or to become your friend, you can increase the odds of this happening by being, as much as possible, like them.

Rapport is gained by employing a variety of techniques. In a sense, you already do many of these things naturally. Conscious appreciation of what you already know how to do will permit you to accomplish your task whenever and with whomever you choose. Rapport has a number of aspects. Each aspect is important, yet it is the cumulative effect that makes it powerful. No single pacing method will automatically establish rapport with another person. However, the cumulative effect of these basic techniques will assist you in creating chemistry with virtually anyone.

10

Rapport through Body Language

This is one of the most powerful influencing techniques you will ever learn. Always remember that people deal with you because they like and trust you. If they don't trust you, they walk away and find someone else who can help them. No longer is this process left to chance.

There are numerous ways to build rapport with another person. To one extent you already do it unconsciously with your friends and associates. This chapter will teach you procedures of achieving rapport using body language.

In this chapter you will learn:

- How to build rapport with another person using your body posture as the primary tool of establishing communication with that person's unconscious
- Special techniques to verify whether you've achieved your purpose
- Exercises that you can use to make sure that these techniques become an automatic part of your behavior

Body language is the first of four rapport-building techniques you will learn which can be used separately but should be used with other techniques presented in subsequent chapters.

Before reviewing the actual techniques, here is an example of the power of unconscious communication. While we were doing a seminar for the Public Relations Association, a typical attitude change occurred among the participants. They were learning these body rapport skills.

On the break, Joan was standing with one hand on her hip and a cup of coffee in the other hand. Her friend, Helen, came out of the seminar, got a cup of coffee, and went over to stand by Joan. Unknown to Joan, Helen unconsciously assumed Joan's exact posture and said something like, "Do you believe this stuff? I think this is just a bunch of junk. It's ridiculous to think that effective people match their styles. I don't believe in this...." Suddenly Helen looked at her friend and at herself, started to laugh, and said, "I'll see you later. I want to get a good seat, so I can learn more."

This response is typical. While working with corporate executives, we'll often get calls 5 minutes after a subordinate or peer leaves their office and they'll say, "I had to stop myself from laughing out loud. It really works, and it's easy and effective! It also saves time."

Preliminaries to Establishing Rapport

Positioning Yourself for a Yes

In a sales presentation, you want your story to influence your potential customer to buy from you. That means that you want to give them what *they* want. In part, this means packaging your product so that it meets their needs while leaving them comfortable with you and assured of your competence. It is often the things you are unaware of that make the difference between success and failure.

Focus of Attention

One of the easiest ways of making someone feel comfortable from the beginning is noticing what makes them comfortable. Imagine for a moment that I wanted to sell you something, and before I came in I said to myself, "Is my hair okay? I hope they like me? Am I standing tall? I want them to know that I am a professional, etc." Where is your focus of attention? That's right! On *yourself*.

When making a sale you want the focus of attention to be on the customer. When you walk into their office or meet them in a restaurant, you should automatically begin paying attention to *them*. There are two results. First, it is easier for you, and second, they feel attended to from the start. Very often, salespeople do their "rap" and don't even know whether or not they have their customer's attention until it is too late.

People always let you know exactly what they need to be comfortable with you. All you have to do is observe. The major premise for the rapport-building materials is summarized by the following rule of thumb: *People like those who are most like themselves*, literally and figuratively.

Matching Body Posture— Mirroring

Matching body posture is one of the easiest and most effective methods of gaining and maintaining rapport. It involves positioning your body in a way which is similar to that of your client—being as much like them as possible. It doesn't mean that you must be a mirror image of the other person, though that is often exactly what it looks like. It does mean that a third person, observing you both, would notice numerous similarities of body posture.

Verify It for Yourself

In order to prove a point, we would like you to determine whether the people in the following stick-figure illustrations are having pleasant or unpleasant conversations. (It would also be worth giving this test to your friends.)

1.

( ) In rapport, pleasant conversation
( ) Out of rapport, unpleasant conversation

2.

( ) In rapport, pleasant conversation
( ) Out of rapport, unpleasant conversation

3.

( ) In rapport, pleasant conversation
( ) Out of rapport, unpleasant conversation

4.

( ) In rapport, pleasant conversation
( ) Out of rapport, unpleasant conversation

The vast majority of people will identify the figures in the first two pictures as probably having amiable or pleasant conversations. Whereas, the second two pictures are identified as uncomfortable. It is interesting to note that similarity of body posture is almost universally identified as "friendly," whereas the lack of similarity is considered unfriendly, or inharmonious.

This intuitive understanding strongly suggests that this very powerful knowledge should be used as often as possible, virtually all the time.

A Reexamination of the Pictures

1.

As you can see, in the first picture two figures are seated at a table. It would be very easy for you to also cross your ankles when you sit down and slightly lean back. The client will be strongly influenced by your similarity of posture and will most often not even notice that posture is the reason.

2.

Two people standing with their arms crossed does not necessarily imply defensiveness or closed-mindedness. People occasionally cross their arms because they're cold; sometimes because it is comfortable. While it is possible that an "attitude" exists, it is usually easier to match the other person's posture and then verify what you think it says about them. Shortly, you will learn a technique to easily lead that person to a different posture.

3.

This pair of postures is generally interpreted as confrontational. The person on the left is thought to be pushing a point, while the other is viewed as defensive. When both of the figures are leaning inward, they are thought to be interested, excited, involved, or showing other similar positive qualities. (Note that a small percentage will view both figures leaning inward as aggressive.)

4.

These figures are thought to be uncomfortable with each other. The total mismatch of body position intuitively causes interpretations revolving around discomfort, distrust, etc.

However, once rapport has been established, body language can shift in and out of sync as the conversation flows. This is normal. As long as you feel comfortable, you probably still have rapport. (There is a procedure for verifying this that will be discussed below.)

Should things bog down, check your body language. If you are not in sync, reestablish posture, and you will likely improve your rapport.

Test It Yourself

As an experiment, have a series of conversations with friends or business associates in which you initially match their body posture for a couple of minutes and then purposely mismatch their body posture by becoming as dissimilar to them as possible. Notice their reactions and the differences in the flow of the conversation. After this, go back to matching and again note the differences—both in yourself and in their reaction.

Most people find that when matched, the conversations are smoother and more relaxed than when body posture is mismatched.

Initially, some people may feel awkward trying this experiment. However, you'll only purposely mismatch a few times to prove to yourself the effects.

You will soon find that your interactions with people are even more comfortable and easygoing as you employ these techniques. These techniques are extraordinarily powerful when used in conjunction with the other rapport enhancers which will be introduced later.

The Best-Laid Plans of...

You may notice that the other person may shift his body posture so that you are no longer matched. Merely wait a few moments, and then casually change your position until you are again somewhat matched. The key is to do it casually and to be as subtle as possible.

Of course, if the other person is fidgety or restless and continually shifts body posture, it would be difficult for you to follow all those changes move by move. A technique called cross matching will help solve this particular situation.

Cross Matching

As was stated earlier, sometimes it is inconvenient or impossible to match the person's posture move-for-move, position-for-position. Trying to precisely match a fidgety person would make your partner aware that you were mimicking him or her and might cause a reduction in or loss of rapport. Subtlety is the key.

Cross matching is a technique which can accomplish both purposes. Essentially, it means matching some other part of the person's body with a dissimilar part of your body. A few examples will serve to explain this procedure:

- If your client is sitting with crossed legs, you can keep your arms crossed while keeping your feet flat on the floor.
- If your client has crossed arms, you can cross your wrists, legs, or ankles.
- A person leaning back on a chair might be cross matched by just leaning to the side and slightly back.
- A hand on the chin can be cross matched by having your hand near your head. As long as your hand is in a similar position, you're okay.
- If someone is sitting with their legs spread apart, you can cross-match by having your arms open.

There are other ways that cross matching can be used effectively. For example, some people like to slowly bounce or move their legs to some internal rhythm. You can match by simply tapping your fingers at the same rate that they move. There is very little chance that they will be consciously aware of what you are doing. Yet, unconsciously, you are maintaining your rapport. An alternative to finger taps would be a very slight, almost unnoticeable, movement of your head. Again, there is very little possibility that the other person will ever be aware of this minute movement. Yet the *unconscious is aware,* and this awareness correlates the rhythm of your two individual movements and maintains or deepens the rapport.

Other Benefits

If you are ever at a meeting where you are to be seen and not heard, these tools are incredibly valuable to you. Let's say that you are a new sales pro and you are going on a sale with a seasoned sales pro. She wants you to follow her lead. By just observing you can usually learn which person is in charge. If you get rapport with that person and match posture rather than sitting back and observing, no one will know you are a novice. The customer will suppose that is just the way you work together, and if you are in the rhythm of the conversation, should anything go your way, you are already in tune with what's going on. You will discover your participation will flow naturally.

It is important to remember that there are many situations in which you may not be the focus of attention. However, you can use your time profitably and establish rapport with someone's (hopefully, the decision maker's) unconscious by subtly matching posture.

Matching body posture to obtain rapport is important. But how do you know that you've achieved your purpose? The next topic gives you a procedure to test for rapport.

Testing for Rapport via Leading

Leading is a testing procedure in which you check whether you have established rapport. After you have matched a person's body posture for a couple of minutes, you might change your posture slightly and wait a few moments (typically 2 to 30 seconds) to see if the other person somehow readjusts his body posture (scratch your nose, or cross your legs, or make some grand gesture). The question is, if you change, does he react to your change by somehow repositioning himself? You will find that when you have rapport with a client or prospect, he, too, will shift something in posture or gesture.

Learn to observe the changes in the other person in response to any rhythm or postural changes you may make. As long as the person responds to your change, however subtle, you have rapport on an unconscious level.

She won't necessarily mirror you, but she will usually somehow readjust herself to you. If not, go back to matching her for a while, then, after a couple of minutes, test again.

It is important to realize that often a half a minute or so will pass before the other person follows your lead by repositioning his or her body. Don't expect the person to immediately follow you. Also realize that it often takes a few minutes of matching before you can successfully lead.

Again, this is something that happens naturally. For example, have you ever noticed in a meeting that if one person yawns you have a sudden urge to yawn? Or if one person coughs, a chain reaction of coughs follows? It's the same type of thing. There will be an urge in the other person to move in harmony with your lead. Whether we consciously bring this to your attention or not, this phenomenon does occur. Watch an audience and observe one person shift; you will notice that others will do the same. Watch the Johnny Carson show or any talk show where the host has good rapport-establishing skills. You will find that this happens all the time.

It Works Even When You Are Aware of It

One day we were working with an executive, and we had very good rapport. At this meeting we were teaching her the skills we are discussing here. Once she knew that rapport means having people move with you, she was greatly amused to find that she was shifting every time one of us moved, and even though she was consciously aware of what was happening, it didn't make a difference. It only verified how well the method worked.

Consciously establish rapport and test it. Shifting will naturally occur many times throughout the conversation when you have rapport. So realize that this is a naturally occurring event. If you discover that your client does not make any change in movement, you probably do not have rapport yet. (Of course, there may be another reason such as physical discomfort of some sort which inhibits their spontaneous movement.) Match posture and pace for another minute and test again.

Remember to test only to establish whether you have rapport. If you do it many times for the heck of it, chances are you will break rapport.

This technique is very effective in reestablishing rapport after interruptions. Many times a phone call, an emergency, a bathroom break, or something else interrupts you, and whereas before you were doing great, now that spell has been broken. When your client or prospect returns to the room or focuses their attention on you, you want to notice their posture, then in that moment, match, wait a minute, and test for rapport while continuing your discussion. Therefore you make sure the rapport is maintained or reestablished.

Leading to Different Emotional States

Leading has other uses besides verifying rapport. As you learned, you can lead a person from one body position to another. The physical shift often results in a corresponding mental shift.

For example, here is a very interesting experiment. Be aware of your own internal, emotional changes as you conduct the following experiment.

1. Be aware of exactly how you are now sitting or standing and your internal feelings associated with that body position.
2. Change your body posture to either more or less relaxed and become aware of your internal changes.
3. Sit ramrod straight, then allow yourself to sink into the chair.

Which position would allow you to carry on a casual conversation? Which body positions do you use in different emotional states? If you associate certain physical states with corresponding psychological states, then consider the ramifications of the following: *You can influence your psychology by your physiology. Your mental and/or emotional states can be influenced by the way you position your body.* This is very useful information which you'll be able to use with yourself and with others.

Here's another demonstration. Now, or at a more appropriate time, stand in a way that allows you to visibly demonstrate how you look when you are really proud of something you did. Allow yourself to swell with pride as you stand or sit tall, shoulders thrown back, a smile on your face. Remember, fully, that good feeling. Relive it. Experience it again.

Now, slump or slouch and note how the intensity of the feeling changes. Then go back to the original position again. We call these postures natural anchors; they allow you to modify an internal state by a change of body posture. If you keep the previous discussion in mind, the other purposes of leading will be easier to understand.

How to Apply Leading in a Sales Situation

If you're speaking with someone you know, and it would be more advantageous if they were in a different mental state, you can match your body to theirs, establish rapport, and shift to a different posture. As a result you will lead them to a different mental state as their own "natural anchors" come into play. You may, for example, wish to lead a person to a relaxed posture and mental state from a stiff posture and state using this method. Or, you might lead someone from a very relaxed posture to one which is normally associated with paying close attention. Remember, postures and mental states go hand in hand.

Assume that you've previously noticed that a client sits up straight and slightly forward when she is enthusiastic. This time, however, the client is in a reclining position. You could initially match the leaning-back position and then lead the client to the position generally associated with enthusiasm.

When you combine this technique with other techniques taught in subsequent chapters, you may be able to exert considerable influence on your client.

Matching Breathing

A very powerful technique for enhancing body rapport is matching breathing rates. Again, the rapport is established below the level of conscious awareness. If matching breathing is combined with other techniques, you have an increased probability of achieving a very deep rapport.

Simply breathe at the same rate as the other person. If you are conversing with them, time your sentences to match their breathing and/or time your breathing to match the inhalations and exhalations of their speech rate. Breathing is a key to the person's natural rhythm and is similar to getting in synchronization with a dance partner.

Watch the rise and fall of the person's chest or shoulders, which of course, correlates with their breath. However, it might be difficult to effectively match breathing with certain people, such as with an asthmatic who breathes very quickly or a long-distance runner who hardly seems to breathe at all. Any time you choose not to match the person breath-for-breath, you have the alternative of employing one of the cross-matching techniques. The movement of your head, finger, or leg to the pace of breathing would provide a good alternative.

It is interesting to note that when you're on the telephone, the only body match that you can make is breathing. Unfortunately, you can't ask, "How are you sitting?" Since so many of our conversations are conducted over the phone, you have the opportunity of improving your telephone personality and effectiveness. Speaking at the same rate (essentially, breathing at the same rate) is another rapport-building technique that is discussed separately.

In conclusion, you have learned that body rapport is a very powerful technique for establishing rapport. People like those who are most like themselves, and this knowledge allows others to feel comfortable with you.

In the next chapter, we will explore these unconscious processes even further.

11
Verbal Pacing and Leading

Have you listened to a person who spoke so slowly that you wanted to help her get the words out of her mouth? How about speaking with someone who spoke so quickly that you felt pushed? Most people have had one or both of those experiences. If someone speaks too slowly for you, you speak too quickly for her. And vice versa. Now both of you have an uncomfortable feeling.

Regional Differences

As you are well aware, there are certain regional language differences between the North and the South. We can gain a considerable edge by noticing the little conversational patterns that make up these differences.

Rate of Speech

Northerners traditionally speak faster than Southerners. A typical Southern reaction is "Why is this person in such a rush?" If a sales pro from the North makes a presentation to a group of Southerners, he or she ought to slow down to match the rate of speech of the group.

This is not mimicking. It is matching the preferences of your client. It would be presumptuous of you to speak in a way you think the client *ought* to prefer. The old saying "When in Rome do as the Romans do" can be translated to the following rule of thumb when applied to speech patterns: *People prefer to listen at the same rate as they speak.* This is an important part of your style in telling your sales story.

One of our friends, named Maria, is employed by an internationally known firm in the customer service department. Maria was born and raised in New York City and had typical New York speech characteristics, which included a Brooklyn accent and a fast speaking rate. She had successfully dealt with Midwestern and Northern accounts but was now assigned to Georgia and Alabama. She was not having the same level of positive responses from her new Southern clients, and one or two had even complained. "Why don't you assign us someone nice?" was the request. She and her boss were getting very frustrated because she performed her duties perfectly. Something was wrong, but no one could put a finger on it. She approached us for assistance.

We listened to Maria's phone conversations and noted that there was a decided difference between her fast-paced, Northern rate of speech and the slower rate of her Southern clients.

It took a little coaching, but Maria was able to consistently slow her rapid (even for New York standards) rate of speech to match those clients who came from the South. Their responsiveness to her increased dramatically and almost immediately. And all she had to do was match the client's speaking rate.

Inflection

Maria was offered an additional enhancement when she was told to slightly raise the inflection in her voice at the end of her sentences. It seems that most Southerners have a slight upward inflection at the end of the sentence—almost as if they were asking a question. Most Northerners, on the other hand, have a downward inflection at the end of the sentence. The original mismatches (rate of speech and inflection), even though seemingly individually insignificant, when added together became significant enough to induce discomfort in the Southern clients.

Shortly thereafter, her accounts had a dramatic increase in responsiveness. Maria simply matched their voice characteristics. One of the clients who had made a complaint actually insisted that she be the only person allowed to handle the account. Maria subsequently went into sales and is immensely successful because she had the backing of such important customers. Maria had learned to tell her story the way her client needed to hear it. She verbally paced them.

We Do It All the Time, Naturally

Verbal pacing is something we do all the time. Have you ever noticed that when someone you care about gets excited, you get excited too? Or perhaps when you are arguing with someone you have rapport with, you find that it's easy to escalate the argument? We can verbally pace someone by matching their rate of speech, tone, volume, pitch, rhythm — all of the things that you can hear. Again, just as when you matched body posture with your client, when you match his speaking rate and patterns, he may find that there is something that he can't put his finger on that he likes about you — it is usually *himself*. Clients hear themselves in you and feel comfortable with you as a result.

We once had a client that had to deal on the phone often. One time she told us of a woman who was a cold, mean person. We asked how she came to that conclusion. She said that the woman on the phone used precise, sharp, rapid tones. However, this client made a judgment about what all of that meant, by labeling this woman as cold. However, she did obtain very relevant information: she listed the voice qualities that her client used. All she had to do was match them. They were quite different from her own, which was slow and whiny with exaggerated endings — anything but clear and precise. The women were different. Not better or worse, just different. It was a total mismatch. All she was told to do was to listen carefully and then match the qualities in the voice that she heard (without the interpretation). The next day when we asked about this cold, unfeeling woman, our client started defending this "warm and gracious" client. The only problem our client had had was a mismatch of pace in voice characteristics.

A New Meaning to "The Customer Is Always Right"

Remember the expression "The customer is always right"? Well, by pacing your customers, you can eliminate any differences. You can make them feel comfortable with you just because your styles match. The effort involved in this is no more than the effort it takes to shift gears in a car. You adjust the gears according to the situation because you know it is necessary to make the car run, or behave well, given its characteristics. You would hardly refuse to shift because the car "ought to want to behave" the way you think it should. You do what is necessary. In conversation, you shift gears for the same reason — it is necessary, and decidedly advantageous.

Throughout our lives we are trying to communicate with others one type of message or another. Effective communication implies a two-way process—you with them and they with you. You can help ensure effective communication by being aware of your speaking rate. If you speak faster than they do, slow down. If you speak slower than they do, speed up. While bringing the client to a yes, we often must overcome initial barriers that would otherwise impede us. Knowing that mismatching speed often causes an unconscious negative reaction, you will find it simple to initially and purposefully match the client.

Leading

As we discussed, pacing is matching the other person's rate of speech. By leading, you can cause him to change his rate while you check for rapport.

For example, when you test for rapport, you change your posture and you discover whether your customer, too, changes her posture. When you have rapport with other people, they will follow you. However, what if matching someone's rapid rate or slow rate is not comfortable. You risk offending your client if you say, "Hey, can you slow down?" An easier method is leading. It's the difference between lassoing someone and demanding he or she join you, and offering an invitation to join you.

The technique is quite simple. After you match your client's rate of speech you can *incrementally* change your rate, either faster or slower, and he or she will usually follow your lead by either speeding up or slowing down to match you. Just like the verification procedures for body rapport, this is another way to test for rapport, as discussed below. Once you've established rapport, your client's unconscious response is to maintain it. This has some interesting potential applications which will be covered shortly. When combined with some of the other rapport-building techniques, you become even more powerful and influential. It is also used as an enhancement to the rapport-building process.

Using Leading in Emergencies

A few years ago, numerous air traffic controllers simultaneously began to search for alternative forms of employment. One of the authors taught in the brokerage industry, and a few years ago, was presenting this pacing and leading concept to a series of new brokers. "Oh, my

God," said one of the men in the group. He explained that he had just realized why he was so effective as an air traffic controller. He had the reputation of always being able to handle difficult, air-emergency situations. He said that whenever a pilot was upset and screaming on the radio, he cooled the pilot down by screaming back for a moment and then progressively lowering his tone of voice and rate of speech. Usually the pilot was brought to a significantly calmer state very quickly. Essentially, he paced the pilot and led him to a calmer state. Until our seminar, he had not realized the mechanics of how he handled these emergencies.

Using Leading in Arguments

We're certain that sometime you have been involved in an argument. Take this scenario: The person you are with is very upset. He is yelling, screaming, and talking a mile a minute. You understand that he is very upset and you're trying to be understanding. And in your gentlest voice tell him to "relax. Let's talk about this calmly."

Have you ever noticed that that usually doesn't work? Usually the response is, "Don't you placate me! Don't patronize me!" And you thought you were being the good guy! This is a classic example of a mismatch. The other person is using loud, rapid voice tones, and you are using calm, slower, softer tones. You may find that you don't want to match by screaming. We can't blame you! This is where you can match in the speed and the tonal qualities. Rather than matching volume, you can match in the power and intensity of your words. Match for a minute and then gradually begin to slow down. You can pace and then lead the other person to a different state.

Testing for Verbal Rapport

In Chapter 10 you learned that you can verify rapport by subtly shifting your body position and then waiting for the other person to adapt his or her body posture to yours. A similar verification process is used here. After initially matching the client for a couple of minutes, you incrementally speed up or slow down your questions or comments. When you have verbal rapport, the client will follow you to that modified rate after a couple of moments. Realize that it may take a few tries before you can successfully lead. The key to the entire procedure is initially matching the other person and then leading.

Applications

This has some interesting ramifications. In Chapter 10, we mentioned that certain body postures facilitate certain mental states. Sitting ramrod straight induces a different mental state than does slouching. Voice rates and tonality work the same way. Certain rates and tonal qualities are associated with certain mental states.

Generating Enthusiasm

You may note that, whenever a certain client is enthusiastic about something, she tends to use a higher tonality and/or a more rapid rate of speech. The client has mental associations of pleasure with that particular rate of speech. If you lead that person to that particular rate in your presentation, you will have increased the probability that the person will be in an enthusiastic mental state. Matching the client's rate of speech initially and leading her to a rate more conducive to better communication allows you to manage the behavior. (You would also be wise to shift your body posture to further lead the client.)

Speeding Up a Slowpoke

Another application of leading would be to assist a person to get to the point more quickly. By merely matching the client and incrementally speeding up your rate of speech, you could get him to state his needs more quickly. This is especially useful when dealing with people who love to have long, drawn out conversations. While this may be acceptable in a social situation, the realization that time is money may cause you to wish that you had a way of politely getting the client to finish with whatever he is saying. Now you have such a way: speed up your rate of speech. The next thing you know, your client is speaking much faster (it may take 10 minutes of leading to get him there). *Make sure you hide your surprise when he finishes his own conversation in less than one lifetime.* However, also be aware that many people associate a very rapid rate of speech with nervousness. This could be detrimental to the conversation. It depends on the client's natural associations. You have the choice to use leading to increase your success ratio.

Often when your speaking pattern is mismatched with that of your client, that person isn't even aware what is happening. The client is either uneasy or uncomfortable or angered by you without knowing why. This may be registered by his or her unconscious and appear as personality conflicts.

12

Insight into the Client's Thinking through Word Choice

You've heard people using phrases such as "It looks good to me" or "It sounds good to me" or "It feels good to me." These phrases, and others like them, provide useful information about people's thinking processes and give you an excellent opportunity to communicate with them more precisely and persuasively.

In the above paragraph, the quoted phrases had visual, auditory, and kinesthetic (feeling) orientations, respectively. Some people think by using visual images in their minds, others may mentally verbalize thoughts, and still others think intuitively in terms of how something feels to them. Each of us has a preference for one or two of these modes of thought. The preference is indicated by the words and phrases used in conversation. People who like to think in pictures use picture words. People who like to think in verbal terms use sound-oriented words. People who like to think kinesthetically (using intuition) use words based on the sense of touch.

We obtain information using the five senses—visual/sight, auditory/sound, kinesthetic/feelings, olfactory/smell, and gustatory/taste. Which we use depends on the situation: if an experience was primarily visual, such as looking at a painting, the memory would tend to have visual dominance. The same is true of the remaining four senses. A concert may have an auditory dominance, while a swim in a pool may be dominated by the kinesthetic mode. Smell and taste are also part of the experience, but they have such a proportionately small place in our culture that we will focus on the three primary senses of sight, sound, and touch.

The Process of Specialization

Over the course of years, most people tend to use one sense more than the others, leading them to think about most things in terms of their favorite sense. The sensory data most preferred determine the nature of our thought processes. We then develop sense-oriented vocabularies. For example, if you generally think by making mental pictures, you will be most often aware of the visual component of your experiences. In recalling an experience, the visual component will be the most vivid and the words that you use to recall that experience would be primarily visual words. Of course, you would also be able to remember the sounds and the feelings associated with the experience, but they tend not to be as strong as the visual component.

The words that we use to describe an experience represent the strongest portion of the memory. That is, if the visual component was the strongest, we would tend to use words and phrases with a visual orientation, such as; "visualize," "perspective," "view," "mental image," "paint a picture," etc. On the other hand, if the sound portion of the memory was most dominant, the words we would use would have an auditory orientation, such as; "listen," "earshot," "tune in," and "clear as a bell." Memories or portions of a memory which have a kinesthetic dominance would be described with words like "grasp," "emotional," "bearable," "enjoyable," and so on.

We Are Most Comfortable with Words Matching Our Thoughts

Since we tend to choose words which most closely correlate with how we think, we will also be most comfortable in dialogue with words and phrases that most closely match our thinking processes. Frequently our choices of words and phrases determine whether we will be understood by others. Word choice may either produce comprehension or confusion on the other person's part and result in either acceptance or rejection of our message.

If you want to communicate clearly with someone who uses a particular mode of thinking, you should use words that match that mode. A speaker's choice of words literally tells you how to best "connect" with him or her. You simply echo that person's preference in your conversation. Try it! You'll be amazed at the degree of improvement in understanding that will occur.

Here Is How It Works

Below is an example of a common statement that might be made in a normal, day-to-day business conversation. It illustrates how you can match another person's thinking processes for positive effects.

Let's assume someone is talking to you about some project he wants to become involved in. The conversation may sound something like this: "I was *looking* over the proposal they submitted, and it *shows* a number of interesting things that have not before been brought to *light*." Your matching response could be one of the following:

- "It certainly *looks* like a good idea to me. How does it *look* to you?"
- "It certainly *sounds* like a good idea to me. What do you have to *say* about it?"
- "It certainly *feels* like a good idea to me. How do you *feel* about it?"

The three responses all mean basically the same thing. Yet, the first response more precisely matches the way the person was presenting the information. By matching his mode of thought, he will realize that you are "seeing things the same way." The second and third responses may cause him to think that you "don't have the picture."

Test It for Yourself

You might consider trying an interesting experiment with some of your friends. Listen carefully to their word modes. If they are relating a story to you in the auditory mode (where most of the words relate to sound), first ask them a few questions about the sound portion of the story and be aware of how easily and quickly they respond. Then, when you ask them a question about the visual and/or kinesthetic aspects of the story, there will probably be a momentary pause while they mentally shift gears.

A smoothly flowing conversation should allow the other person to continue with the story without constantly having to shift gears from one mode to another. Should someone continually ask them questions requiring this mental shift, one of two things happens: the responses may shift to the new aspect, thereby matching the questions that are being asked, or more probably, the person may become slightly annoyed that he or she is unable to tell the story effectively, feeling "interrupted" somehow. As a professional communicator, it is in your best interest to allow people to talk comfortably with you.

Another Test of This Technique

Here is another interesting experiment that you may wish to try with a few of your friends. The real estate sales professionals will really like this one, yet everyone should be able to benefit from it. Talk to a friend on the phone or in person, saying that you wish to briefly describe three homes or apartments. Ask your friend to pretend to be in the market for a new home, and because of time constraints, he or she can only visit one of the places described. You will be a real estate agent who is describing the three houses, using the descriptions that follow. Pause for a few seconds after you read each description to allow time for your friend to think about the information. *Your friend must make a choice among the three.*

The First House

There is a house which I'm sure you would like to see. The first house is in a beautiful neighborhood and is very picturesque. Even the doorbell has a unique design. The rooms look large and have the right colors. You can really consider yourself living here as you see that this would be a wonderful place to live. If you go to the balcony, you can see some really nice scenery. I'm sure you'll perceive this as an excellent buy.

The Second House

Yet, there is another house that I'm sure you would like to hear about. This second house is in a quiet neighborhood and is of very sound construction. Even the doorbell has a nice ring to it. The rooms have good acoustics. You can really consider yourself living here as you say to yourself that this sounds like a wonderful place to live. If you go to the balcony, you can hear the birds chirping and the sound of the breeze. I'm sure you'll tell yourself that this is an excellent buy.

The Third House

There is one more house that I'm sure you would find satisfying. This third house is in a warm neighborhood and is very solidly built. Even the doorbell gives a welcome feeling. The rooms are spacious and comfortable. You can really consider yourself living here as you sense that this would be a wonderful place to live. If you go to the balcony, you can feel the warm sun and a light breeze. I'm sure you'll feel that this is an excellent buy.

Ask your friends which house they would choose. Also ask them if they disliked a particular house. The results are interesting. Even though the same house is described in three different sensory modes, most people will have a preference, sometimes very strong, for one of the descriptions. Even more interesting is the fact that a number of people will actually dislike one of the houses. The descriptions were kept similar, and only the sensory word mode was changed. The house that a person likes has high probability of matching his or her own thinking preference. The house which is least liked usually belongs to the word-mode system that person makes the least use of.

Two Scripts

We often demonstrate the power of word modes to groups (usually 50 people or more) by asking two of the participants to read the following scripts. They leave the room to practice reading it a few times so that the only difference between one script and the other is a few words. They are instructed to make the volume, tones, emphasis, etc., as identical as possible. While they are practicing, the audience is instructed that, when they have heard both of the scripts, they must choose the script that they believe gives Mary the better chance of continuing the conversation with John. The audience is given no additional information. The two people return and read the following scripts.

Reading 1

MARY: I just came across something that looks interesting, and if you have a moment, I'd like to show it to you.

JOHN: Sounds interesting. I'd like to hear some more.

MARY: Well, I just saw something which shows that they should improve in the next few months.

JOHN: What do you mean? I've heard that they are in really bad shape.

MARY: Yet it shows that we should know about a change in the near future, which is why you...(*John interrupts.*)

JOHN: My gut reaction is that things will stay the same.

MARY: What have you seen to make you think that way? I perceive the case is very positive.

JOHN: Well, I've been hearing just the opposite.

MARY: Look, I want to show you a few things which should give you a better picture.

A momentary pause is made between the readings.

Reading 2

MARY: I just came across something that looks interesting, and if you have a moment, I'd like to show it to you.

JOHN: Sounds interesting. I'd like to hear some more.

MARY: Well, I just heard something which states that they should improve in the next few months.

JOHN: What do you mean? I've heard that they are in really bad shape.

MARY: Yet it states that we should know about a change in the near future, which is why you... (*John interrupts.*)

JOHN: My gut reaction is that things will stay the same.

MARY: What have you heard to make you think that way? I feel the case is very positive.

JOHN: Well, I've been hearing just the opposite.

MARY: Listen, I want to tell you a few things which should give you a better feeling.

The audience is then polled regarding in which of the two scripts gives Mary a better chance of continuing the conversation. Invariably, the majority of the audience will pick Reading 2. When asked about the difference between the scripts, they usually make comments to the effect that Reading 1 was more confrontational and aggressive and that Mary was unresponsive, unwilling to listen, uninterested in John, uncaring, etc.

In Reading 2 Mary is usually identified as being more supportive, understanding, attentive, responsive, caring, and interested.

After this audience analysis, the demonstrators read the scripts again. However, the person playing Mary reads the equivalent sentences from the first and second scripts back-to-back. The audience is told to listen to the difference between the two scripts; they are usually absolutely amazed that the mere change of word modes (mismatched in Reading 1 and matched in Reading 2) makes that much difference. The change in response occurs outside of conscious awareness.

There are only eight words that are changed from one script to the other, yet these words will cause about 95 percent of an audience to react adversely to Reading 1 and favorably to Reading 2. (These results have held true with over 10,000 people.)

The script is repeated on the next page with the key words emphasized. In both situations John's statements are identical. Mary uses mismatched words in Reading 1 (John uses auditory words, and Mary continues to use visual words) and matched words in Reading 2, where Mary immediately adapts her words to John's speaking style after the first sentence. As you will see, the change of eight words makes all the difference in the world.

Mary's Script in Reading 1 versus Reading 2

MARY 1: I just came across something that looks interesting, and if you have a moment, I'd like to show it to you.

MARY 2: I just came across something that looks interesting, and if you have a moment, I'd like to show it to you.

JOHN: *Sounds* interesting. I'd like to *hear* some more.

MARY 1: Well, I just *saw* something which *shows* that they should improve in the next few months.

MARY 2: Well, I just *heard* something which *states* that they should improve in the next few months.

JOHN: What do you mean? I've *heard* that they are in really *bad shape*.

MARY 1: Yet it *shows* that we should know about a change in the near future, which is why you...(*John interrupts.*)

MARY 2: Yet it *states* that we should know about a change in the near future, which is why you...(*John interrupts.*)

JOHN: My *gut reaction* is that things will stay the same.

MARY 1: What have you *seen* to make you think that way? I *perceive* the case is very positive.

MARY 2: What have you *heard* to make you think that way? I *feel* the case is very positive.

JOHN: Well, I've been *hearing* just the opposite.

MARY 1: *Look,* I want to *show* you a few things which should give you a better *picture*.

MARY 2: *Listen,* I want to *tell* you a few things which should give you a better *feeling*.

As a final note, it is important to realize that the dialogue was purposely left in a slightly confrontational mode in order to fully verify the power of this subconscious communication procedure. See Chap. 16 for a more thorough discussion of confrontations.

What to Listen For

It is easy to determine a person's preferred thinking mode by listening to him or her attentively. The visual person may use words and phrases like "I see what you mean," "It looks good to me," "pretty as a picture," "tunnel vision," "plain to see," etc. The auditorily oriented person says things like "Sounds good to me," "clear as a bell," "speak to you soon," and so on. Phrases such as "cool, calm, and collected," "keep in touch," "boils down to," and "get a handle on" are often used by the kinesthetic person. (A more complete list is provided at the end of the chapter.)

You'll also note that people will use two word modes in the same conversation, such as "I've been feeling pretty good because I can see myself making real progress as I plough through these reports, which have obviously been piling up." In this sentence both kinesthetic words (*feeling, plough, piling*) and visual words (*see, obviously*) were used. You may also note that the person also rarely uses auditory words. In this case the visual and kinesthetic words would be considered the prime systems, while auditory words would be the least-used mode.

Imagine a sales situation where a highly auditory salesperson makes a presentation to a highly visual client or prospect. The probability of the sale is significantly reduced because each is, in a sense, speaking a different language. Communication is hampered. The mismatch of word preferences in the presentation virtually guarantees that the client will be confused and the sale will be lost. However, if the same salesperson were able to effectively use the client's preferred thinking mode, then the probability of a sale would be greatly enhanced.

People Really Use All Three Modes

Does this mean that a person *only* uses one or two systems and *never* uses the third mode? Of course not. Some experiences are so specifically oriented to one mode that a person may recall that memory in their least-used system. For example, the person who least prefers the auditory speaking mode might use auditory words as she recalls a phone conversation, a concert, or a radio show in which the auditory component was the most dominant.

Knowing When to Use Which Mode

Some people use one type of word choice for certain situations and a different mode for others. There are also some individuals who are comfortable with all three systems and mix their systems regularly. It is this last group of people who are often key communicators and are able to easily interact with large numbers of people. As you use these word preferences and extend your own ability to shift gears among the modes, you can become a member of this key communicator group. After just a little practice, you'll be able to match modes with another person easily and automatically.

Other Applications

Matching word modes has applications in virtually every area of our lives. There are probably individuals you know who are difficult to communicate with — because they either cannot see what you're saying, or hear what you're saying, or grasp what you're saying. Your job is to determine their preferred word modes and match them. That simple effort will make a major difference. Your conversations with your friends, family, business associates, and clients will be significantly improved.

Remember, *people like those who think most like themselves.* An old saying applies here: "Birds of a feather flock together." These key word modes tell you what "plumage" to wear in conversation so that your dialogue is more effective.

Matching your words to those of other people significantly enhances the communication process. Mismatching the word modes often increases the barriers that can exist between people. Literally and figuratively, matching word modes allows you to communicate for positive effects.

How a Stockbroker Used Word Choices to His Advantage

One of our acquaintances was a stockbroker who decided to try this technique with some of his prospective clients. He later recounted to us that he had one prospect who was highly visual and who rarely used auditory words. The prospect was trying to decide with which of two firms he should open an account.

His presentation went something like this: "I'm sure that you'll be able to *see* all of the benefits of using my firm. Our reputation is *spotless* and we take pride in *showing* our clients many other *attractive* investment alternatives that may not otherwise be *obvious.*"

He continued by making a comment about the competition. "I'm sure," he said, "that the other broker you are considering has also *said* many good things about his firm. His *suggestions* may be along the same lines, and he may even *discuss* similar investment alternatives with you that you may not have *heard* about."

The prospect took some time to think it over and called back about an hour later. He said something akin to the following: "I've thought it over and realize that you really have a *clear perspective* on my situation. I *foresee* a good long-term relationship. The other fellow just doesn't seem to have a good *picture* of my financial needs."

This switch in firms happened all because the stockbroker matched word modes when he referred to himself and his firm and mismatched word modes when referring to the other firm. This is the power of knowing the other person's thinking mode.

How One Sales Professional Used It with Her Sales Manager

The vital importance of matching word modes also applies to other areas of our lives such as work relationships. For example, one sales professional realized that she and her local sales manager were having major communication difficulties, not because of differences in outlook, but because they used different word modes. She and her sales manager were literally speaking in different languages—he was highly auditory while she was very kinesthetic.

She realized that in the past he was "unable to *grasp* the idea." He often couldn't get a sense of the situation and always demanded "*tell* me more." Yet no matter how often she tried to give him the feel or the essence of her thoughts, he requested more detailed information. The situation had lead to strained relations.

When she modified her word mode pattern to match his, they found that they were able to agree on many things. Eventually, she also taught him how to use word modes so that he could match her word modes as well as the modes of the other sales representatives. They found that they could both communicate easily using visually oriented words and now find that their relationship is happier as a direct result. These are the same kinds of effects you want to achieve in the sales situation with your customers as well as with your boss. (And, take our word for it, it works at home too.)

Unspecified Words

In discussing word modes we need to mention "unspecified" word modes such as *think, consider, believe,* and *verify.* They are called unspecified because they do not correlate to any sensory-based word mode. They are generic words that cut across all five senses. These are words that can be used with virtually any word-mode system. You can use unspecified words when you first meet the person or until you determine which is his or her preferred word mode. At that point you switch into that preferred mode so that you deepen your rapport and enhance your effectiveness. Of course, here and there you will find a person who mostly uses the unspecified word mode.

It is better to use unspecified words than to mismatch. At least you remain somewhat neutral. The ideal is to match word modes.

You could also use unspecified words when you go into a committee meeting or make a presentation to a group. Start with unspecified words and then mix in word modes from visual, auditory, and feeling modes. When presenting to large audiences we suggest you use a lot of visual aides in order to take care of the visual members of the audience. Our words will emphasize auditory and kinesthetic word modes to take care of everyone else. Often, audience participation will allow the auditory participants to hear a good dialogue, while getting the audience to do something—such as writing or moving around—will attend to the kinesthetic members of the group.

For example, here is a mixed use of word modes in a typical presentation: "As you *look* at the graph, it *suggests* that things are beginning to *turn around*. The graph *presents* a series of interesting alternatives that we can *discuss* in greater detail. My *sense* is that the above *data on the screen* need to be *weighed* carefully. Let's *talk* about it more."

This brief demonstration above shows you how to mix all of the modes to suit your audience. Certain key points may be worth repeating three times (once in each mode) so that the entire audience is able to hear and understand your point. By allowing the audience, committee, prospect, or customer to see what you are referring to, you allow them to get a better feel for the issue at hand. If you analyze this paragraph carefully, you will see that we are employing the same concepts to allow you to feel comfortable with the concept that we are currently discussing.

Remember that it is extremely rare for an individual to use only one mode exclusively. Most people regularly employ two modes with relative ease. One mode may dominate, but there is usually a secondary mode which they can also easily use in a conversation. Consequently, when speaking to such people, feel comfortable using the two systems that they habitually employ and avoid using the one that they use least.

The following table contains a list of sensory-oriented words and phrases. We suggest that you practice your presentations in each of the three primary modes so that you can maximize your effectiveness and create an atmosphere of rapport and understanding.

Sensory and Unspecified Words

Visual	Auditory	Kinesthetic	Unspecified
see	sound	feel	think
picture	hear	grasp	decide
appear	mention	firm	motivate
outlook	inquire	pressure	understand
imagine	scream	grip	plan
focus	tune	moves	know
perception	shrill	flow	consider
foresee	oral	stress	advise
vista	earful	callous	deliberate
looks	listen	warm	develop
clear	ring	numb	create
observe	resonate	dull	manage
horizon	loud	hold	repeat
scope	vocal	affected	anticipate
notice	remark	emotional	indicate
show	discuss	solid	admonish
scene	articulate	soft	activate
watch	say	active	prepare
overview	announce	bearable	allow
angle	audible	charge	permit
aspect	boisterous	concrete	direct
clarity	communicate	foundation	discover
cognizant	converse	hanging	ponder
conspicuous	dissonant	hassle	determine
examine	divulge	heated	resolve
glance	earshot	hunch	meditate
hindsight	enunciate	hustle	believe
illusion	interview	intuition	cogitate
illustrate	noise	lukewarm	judge
image	proclaim	motion	evaluate
inspect	pronounce	muddled	reckon
obscure	report	panicky	imagine
obvious	roar	rush	contemplate
perspective	rumor	sensitive	assume
pinpoint	screech	set	conceptualize
scrutinize	silence	shallow	conceive
sight	speak	shift	influence
sketchy	speechless	softly	accept
survey	squeal	stir	prove
vague	state	structured	depend
view	tell	support	communicate
vision	tone		comprehend

Sensory Phrases

Visual	Auditory	Kinesthetic
an eyeful	blabbermouth	all washed up
appears to be	clear as a bell	boils down to
bird's-eye view	clearly expressed	chip off the old block
catch a glimpse of	call on	come to grips with
clear-cut	describe in detail	cool, calm, collected
dim view	earful	firm foundation
eye to eye	express yourself	floating on thin air
flashed on	give an account of	get a handle on
get a perspective on	give me your ear	get a load of this
get a scope on	heard voices	get the drift of
hazy idea	hidden message	get your goat
in light of	hold your tongue	hand-in-hand
in person	idle talk	hang in there
in view of	idle talk (tongue)	heated argument
looks like	inquire into	hold it
make a scene	keynote speaker	hold on
mental image (picture)	loud and clear	hothead
mind's eye	power of speech	keep your shirt on
naked eye	purrs like a kitten	lay cards on table
paint a picture	outspoken	light-headed
photographic memory	rap session	moment of panic
plainly see	rings a bell	not following you
pretty as a picture	state your purpose	pull some strings
see to it	tattletale	sharp as a tack
short-sighted	to tell the truth	slipped my mind
showing off	tongue-tied	smooth operator
sight for sore eyes	tuned in/out	so-so
staring off into space	unheard of	start from scratch
take a peek	utterly	stiff upper lip
tunnel vision	voiced an opinion	stuffed shirt
up front	within hearing range	topsy-turvy
well-defined	word for word	underhanded

Just as each person has a preferred thinking pattern, you'll find that members of the same profession share a common jargon. It develops naturally as people create verbal shorthand, or jargon, to quickly and efficiently express themselves.

This provides you with an opportunity to match them on yet another level by using words that they are comfortable with. However, be extraordinarily careful about using your own professional jargon with them. That is one of the surest ways to confuse and thereby lose rapport and trust.

Matching the Customer's Jargon in Various Fields

We've scanned literature from various professions, searching for buzzwords that seem to be common to the industry. Try to make presentations using *their* words to explain *your* concepts. You may find it helpful to highlight the words that you can use. The following is a series of explanations that could be used by a stockbroker with clients from various professions. The stockbroker is suggesting that the client sell certain stocks because they are poor investments. (We took a few liberties and exaggerated the word usage for the purpose of the demonstration and for pure enjoyment. You would want to be more subtle.)

To a person already familiar with brokerage jargon. "I've reviewed your portfolio and think you should consider doing some *swaps* because some of the items are *fundamentally* and *technically* weak. I think that my ideas to strengthen your *portfolio* will make sense."

To an accountant. "I've *analyzed* your holdings and think that you should consider some changes. The *figures* show that some of your holdings are weak. When you *add up* my ideas, I'm sure that you'll agree."

To an architect. "I've analyzed your holdings and see some need to change the *structure* of the portfolio. I've a few ideas that will give you a better *foundation* and better *support*. As you review the *blueprint,* I'm sure you'll agree that these are some good ideas."

To a doctor. "I've examined your portfolio and discovered some stocks that ought to be *cut* from your current holdings because they are *terminal*. [We couldn't resist this one.] The *prognosis* is good. Once we deal with the issue, your portfolio will *recover*."

To a florist. "I've looked at your holdings and find that the *root* of your problems is that certain stocks are *wilting*. We have to *nip* the problem in the *bud* by *cutting away* some excesses. Once you think about it, I'm sure that you'll like the new *arrangement*."

Following is a list of occupation-related words we have gathered from a variety of fields. Normally, you will find that your customer will use words that relate to his or her field, and these indicate preferences. Listen for them. This following list is only suggestive; there is no substitute for noticing the word preferences of your particular customer.

Accountant		
forms	accounts	clients
cash flow	tax bracket	taxes
shelter	IRS	revenue
actuarial	analyze	accrete
depreciate	amortize	invest
conservative	conservator	facts
figures	projections	estimates
accurate	inaccurate	adds up
precise	recoup	

Architect		
design	structure	draw
precise	stress	blueprint
support	buttress	wall
floor	ceiling	level
depth	height	weight
dimensions	proposal	model
mock-up	lines	flow

Attorney		
evaluation	procedures	judge
legal	case	evidence
document	determine	system
disclaimer	claim	complaint
jury	defend	plaintiff
trial	mis/mal/non-feasance	

Insurance Executive

sales	accident	liability
property	health	savings
actuarial	statistics	life
term	annuity	mortality
loan	insure	premium
risk	exposure	

Computer Engineer

data	crash	field
structure	entry	subroutine
analysis	logic	structure
verify	design	flow
dimensions	proposal	model
test	generate	report

Businessperson

proposal	measurement	image
objectives	cash	cash flow
profit	deficit	management
equity	inventory	responsibilities
supervision	control	information
systems	labor	benefit
inventory	turnover	personnel
margin	tested	tried and true
performance		

Small Businessperson

inventory	taxes	sales
expand	profit	loss
turnover	cash flow	employees

Educator

measurement	testing	objectives
guidance	self-image	self-actualization
study	thesis	over/under achiever
behavior	academics	cognitive
effective	projection	aids
counselors	specialist	dissertation
aim	outcome	motivation
follow up	procedure	foils

Physician

ill	sick	surgery
diagnosis	medication	examination
health	prognosis	practice
recover	medical	insurance
cut	scalpel	cancer
specialist	specialization	practitioner
body	disease	prevention
prescribe	reaction	allergic

Florist or Farmer

root	grow	flower
bud	dry up	wilt
shrivel	rot	fade
fragrant	odor	moist
light	petal	arrangement
bouquet	smell	mix
assortment	fertile	gift
sort	transplant	budding
process	bloom	blossom
arrange	stem	branch
fresh	firm	texture
nip in the bud	germinate	seed
fertilize	turnover	exposure
aromatic		

Engineer		
circuit	design	structure
math	stress	blueprint
dimensions	proposal	plan
model	mock-up	demonstration
test	procedure	logic
build	create	implement
precise	tested	

13

The Eyes
Are Windows
to the Mind

Eye movements are an important clue to how well your sales story is doing the job, and they also provide insight (literally and figuratively) into the thinking process.

The Eyes Do More than Just See

One of the many discoveries in recent years is that the eyes are more than mere receptors for visual data. Eye movements are used to help access or obtain neurological data, which include our memories, that is, the physical movement of the eye is actually part of the brain's memory and thinking procedure when the brain is processing certain types of information. Eye movement is part of our brain's "hard-wiring" and indicates what is going on during the thinking process. It gives an indication of how human beings work with their minds even though they are not aware of revealing this information.

Eye movements are connected with the thinking process and are a window into a person's mind. Watching someone's eye movements allows you to know whether he or she is retrieving or using visual, auditory, or kinesthetic data. This valuable information allows you to tailor your sales story even more precisely to your client, especially when it is combined with the word modes that you learned in the previous chapter and some of the other techniques presented elsewhere in the book. An extraordinarily powerful presentation results from knowing how to interpret eye movements.

Universal Eye Patterns

Everyone in the world employs the following eye patterns. In the scientific literature they are called Universal Eye Patterns. In the next few pages you will see figures such as [●◉] , [◉◉] , and [◉●] , which are designed to correlate to the illustration below. They represent the direction of eye movement of the person you are observing.

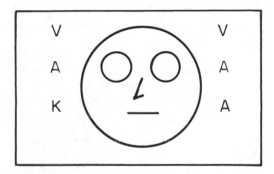

Visual Eye Pattern

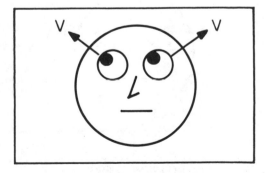

Most people picture things by looking up—either left or right. If you are talking with someone who regularly looks up, you would want to use visually oriented words. These words would most closely match that person's thinking mode.

Blank Stare

The blank or defocused [⊙⊙] stare doesn't mean "nobody's home"; it merely lets you know that the other person is visualizing something. He or she may be daydreaming. Again, you would use visual words.

Auditory Eye Pattern

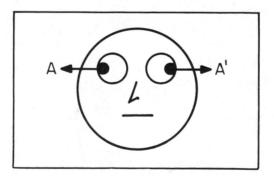

You may notice that some people may look side to side as they try to respond to a question. They are processing in the auditory mode. A person looking horizontally to his or her right [⊃⊙] or left [⊙⊂] is probably deciding what to say next.

Some people, such as former President Richard Nixon, continually look from side to side. *Shifty-eyed* has been applied to some of them, but it is not always an accurate description of what is going on in their minds.

If you notice this pattern, it would help your story to use auditory word modes. Saying things like "Let's discuss this further" would more precisely match their communication processes.

Kinesthetic Eye Pattern

A right-handed person looking down and to his right [○○] is usually experiencing a feeling at that moment. You would do well to use kinesthetic words.

Self-Talk Eye Pattern

A right-handed client who is looking down and to her left [👁👁] is often either repeating your question to herself or debating something internally. In other words, she is talking to herself at that moment.

"What do you say to yourself as you think about this issue?" would typically cause the other person to look [👁👁] down and to her left as she recalls the details. Of course, she may not be consciously aware of it. Yet if you asked her something like "What were you debating?" she would probably easily answer. Some clients might be surprised that you "knew" that they were debating with themselves. Others will say "I wasn't debating anything. I was thinking about something." Six of one, half dozen of the other. Meanwhile, you would be able to use auditory word modes to match their internal thought processes.

Using This Information in Day-to-Day Conversations

In face-to-face conversations you can match your word modes to correlate with clients' or prospects' eye movements. Visual word modes would include words such as *sight, vision, outlook, focus, notice,* and *watch* and would be used when you saw eye patterns of [👁👁] , [👁👁] , or [👁👁] .

Auditory word modes would be used when you observed [👁👁] , [👁👁] , or [👁👁] used with regularity. Use words such as *sounds, hear, mention, listen, vocal,* and *articulate.*

[👁👁] would remind you to use kinesthetic word modes in the sense of touch to match their thought modes. The words that would be most effective would include words such as *feel, grasp, flow, firm,* and *solid.*

Visual

For example, if a person says, [👁👁] "I need to think about that," you might respond by saying, "What can I *show* you to give you a clearer *picture?*"

You know that they were employing pictures as part of the thought process. By saying that they need to think about something, they indicate a need to mentally see something different. Maybe you can supply the missing piece to complete this mental jigsaw puzzle. Visual word modes would also be used when people use phrases such as [👁👁] "It seems a bit fuzzy," [👁👁] "I can't quite see what you mean," [👁👁] "It looks good to me," etc. In these situations use visual words.

Auditory

A person says, [oo] "I need to think about that." You might respond by saying, "What can I *tell* you so the idea *sounds* better?"

You know that the person is using the auditory thinking pattern by the eye patterns consistently employed. As indicated in Chap. 12, some people prefer to process information in the auditory mode. Consequently, you should match their preferred thinking mode. After you ask, "What can I *tell* you so the idea *sounds* better?" the client might say, "Well, I need to discuss some of the major points a bit more." "Which points?" you ask. [oo] "Earlier you said something that I didn't understand. Perhaps you can explain this again." Of course, you give the answers necessary.

Kinesthetic

The client says, [oo] "I need to think about that." You might respond by saying, "What can I *do* to give you a better *feeling?*" Just as before, you are matching the client's thoughts with your questions.

Asking these questions as suggested will not necessarily give you the exact answer you need to go for the close. It does provide you with information and a direction. Asking such questions and watching the other person's eye patterns are significantly better that not doing anything at all, or even worse, accidentally speaking in a different sensory system, which would probably confuse the client even further and virtually guarantee the loss of the sale.

You can be aware of eye patterns to enhance your conversational abilities, or you can be aware of them just as a matter of interest. However, using this information makes you more effective in your communications.

It's a Bit More Complicated

We can now mention a few refinements in the use of this system of eye patterns. Sometimes a person will look in a direction and use a word mode that do not seem to correlate, such as, [oo] "It doesn't feel right." That's normal. We'll occasionally remember a particular picture or sound and be most aware of the feelings associated with that picture as in the above example. In this case you have a choice of using visual or kinesthetic words. Your better shot is probably with the visual word because the feeling was derived from the picture. Something in the picture wasn't quite right, which resulted in a less-than-positive feeling. "What would you like to see?" would probably get you the information you need to close the sale.

A person might have looked down [⊙⊙] or sideways [⊙⊙] and used a visual word mode. Match the eye movement with your words, if possible. If that doesn't give you the information you want, match the word mode. In either case, you'll increase your probability of obtaining the knowledge necessary to effectively deal with this particular client. Even though there are complications to the basic theme, you'll find that people usually correlate their words to their eye movements.

Some Additional Applications

The potential applications for using this information are much more extensive than that presented in this chapter. They include creating a window into the thinking process so that the process itself can be modified or replicated. These patterns connect to the actual thinking sequence, which is called a strategy. You must be thoroughly familiar with the eye movement process before you can use strategies as presented in Chap. 12. A good example is the mental procedure used by people who can spell very well.

There is a significant difference between the mental sequences used by effective spellers versus those used by poor spellers. Good spellers make pictures of their words, while poor spellers try to sound out the words. In English, words often don't look as they sound. Therefore, a speller needs a good visual memory to spell well. The spelling strategy, a mental visualization technique, can be taught to poor spellers usually within a half hour. The result is that they, too, become effective spellers. In selling, this rather simple application implies that thought processes can be learned and then taught to others.

For those of us in sales, this means that we can learn precisely how a person sequences information and then make our sales presentation match the client's mindset by using his preferred sequence (discussed in Chap. 17) as well as the words he is employing internally. As a result, it seems as if the client is convincing himself to buy your offering. This is the power of matching. People then virtually "sell themselves" because of the inherent persuasiveness of your presentation. You are using their own "convincer" strategy by echoing it back to them.

In summary, a person's eye movements are correlated to her word modes (i.e., sensory word preferences). When a person looks up and thinks in pictures, the tendency is for her to speak in visual words. When her eyes move to the side, she is thinking in sounds and/or words.

You may confidently expect her to express her statements in auditory words. Finally, when looking down and to her right, she is thinking intuitively (in feelings) and her speech will be heavily laden with feeling- and touch-oriented words.

I'm sure that you can see [◐◑] *the potential usefulness of this information and can* tell [◐◑] *yourself that you would like to use this information in your daily personal and professional interactions and that you will have a good* feeling [◐◑] *when you become aware of just how easy it is to do.*

14
The Power of Positive Emphasis

Such is the effect of language. Our thinking is influenced by what other people say, and their thinking is directed by what we say. In this sense, selling is a word game. Words have the power to influence. But you must know the rules of the game, and speaking in positive language is one of the very important rules.

You have the ability to choose the words you use. You can direct someone's thoughts toward an idea, or away from an idea. It's up to you.

Becoming Aware of Negative Emphasis

Try this experiment: Don't think of a pink elephant. Do not *think* of a *pink elephant*. You *had* to think of the pink elephant before you could dismiss the thought. Try it out with your friends. Many of them will smile as they realize that they couldn't not think of one.

Try to avoid responding to the next question: "Can you think about the Statue of Liberty?" Your mind had to automatically focus, however briefly, on the Statue of Liberty, or you didn't read the question. Questions create a vacuum that the mind must fill with an answer. This fact can't be denied, and it is very useful in sales. There is power in a question—much more power than most people realize.

What Jack and Jill Didn't Do

Here is a nursery rhyme that will sound really odd: "Jack and Jill didn't go up the hill to fetch something other than a pail of water. Jack didn't fall down and break his crown, and Jill didn't come tumbling after." This is a weird way to tell a story. But many of us do the equivalent all the time. Important points can be made from these examples:

- Language directs the thinking that is the basis of communication.
- You *must* respond to a question.
- Language must be formulated with positive wording for it to have the intended effect.

Don't Worry

What do you do when someone tells you, "There is nothing to worry about"? Chances are that you worry about what it is that you shouldn't be worrying about. Someone may say, "There's no need to concern yourself about this." Most of us automatically want to learn more about what we're not supposed to be concerned about, thereby becoming concerned.

How to Get What You *Don't* Want

We take for granted that when we say what we don't want we will get what we do want. But it actually works in the opposite way. We get what we ask for, and when we use negative language, we get what we don't want.

What happens when you tell a toddler, "Don't spill the milk"? Of course, they spill the milk. Mom and Dad seldom recognize that the child actually did what she or he was asked to do. The brain perceives negatively worded phrasing without the negative. The child actually hears "Spill the milk." This is odd but true. *Within an average day, you will notice that most people state what they don't want instead of what they do want.*

Consider the effect on a child of "Don't drop the glass." The child had to remember what it is like to drop a glass and then, before it's too late, insert the command "do not." The child will drop the glass because of the mental image that had to be recalled. Children hear many other such negative statements: "Don't cross the street." "Don't fall down." "Don't forget." "Don't do this." "Don't do that." "I don't want you to...," etc.

Your packaging of words and phrases will affect the outcome of your communication in a very direct way. We find that successful communicators are never unintentionally negative in their wording.

The Effect of Negative Embedded Commands

When you resort to this simple language pattern, you are actually telling them to do what you don't want. In each of the above negative phrasings, plus hundreds of others, the negative statement, also known as a negative embedded command, slightly stacked the deck in favor of an outcome opposite to that desired. Parents, teachers, bosses, and customers get angry and frustrated because people "never seem to listen." As you realize by now, it's not that people fail to listen but rather that people do as they are told, unconsciously ignoring the negative commands.

We have a saying: "The way you holler at the mountain is the way your echo comes back." When people resist your persuasive efforts, one of the keys to becoming more persuasive is to speak to them in positively phrased words and phrases rather than in negatively packaged language.

We must mention again that talking in positives is a crucial part of your story telling tool kit. You need to talk in positives to shape your story to fit the client's mindset. You clearly want to avoid tripping on your own shoelaces, which is exactly what happens when you talk in negatives.

People in general have difficulty filtering out the negatives. Our minds tend to be quite literal and must create mental images of what we're not supposed to do before those images can be negated. (There is controversy in the scientific community about whether an image can ever be negated.) A rule of thumb is: The unconscious mind deletes negatives. Another way of thinking about it is that the unconscious mind tends to be quite literal.

Positive Embedded Commands

Consider the difference in imagery when the alternative commands (positive embedded commands) are used: "Carry the glass carefully" versus "Don't drop the glass"; "Walk carefully" versus "Don't fall down"; "Remember to...." versus "Don't forget to..."; "Stay on this side of the street" versus "Don't cross the street." Each statement leads to a different mental image. It is your choice which image you will lead people to. Words are very powerful. They direct thoughts and memories. Thoughts and memories, in turn, influence attitudes, behaviors, beliefs, and actions.

"Don't Forget" versus "Remember"

Have you ever gone to the supermarket to get one thing in particular and said to yourself, "Don't forget the milk, don't forget the milk," and found that when you returned the only thing you had forgotten was the milk. Try saying, "Remember the milk," next time, and you'll be in for a pleasant surprise.

This same principle is used in selling. Preface what you want your customer to recall with "Remember x feature" or "Remember to call back," as opposed to "Don't forget x feature" or "Don't forget to call." Your words are very powerful and you get what you ask for, so remember to ask for what you want.

It's an insidious process. Adults subconsciously process the information in the manner just described. Simultaneously, they are consciously aware of what you really mean to say. Essentially, when we introduce conflicting messages into our listener's thinking, we defeat our own purposes.

Some Unfortunately Familiar Examples

The phrase "Don't feel bad" is an example of this contradictory process. Consciously we know that the statement was designed to assist or sympathize. It's a common statement, and we know what it should mean. However, unconsciously, "feel bad" was the command. Now there is a contradiction. After the first few times maybe no reaction is noted. After we have heard it a few more times, we unconsciously move away from this person — somehow we feel worse than usual around him or her.

The same thing happens when we talk to clients. We tell them not to worry. Therefore, they worry. A salesperson who proudly lets a customer know that there are no problems with the service department often gets a customer who is now confident that there are problems with the service department. What would be the effect if the client were very concerned with good service?

An Experiment with Mike

We once tried an experiment on a member of a training group who refused to believe the power of the spoken word. Mike was convinced that he was able to control his mind and that the statements of other people could not affect him. He gave us permission to experiment. Over the course of an hour, a few of the group members would periodically walk up to Mike and tell him, "Don't forget to bring your *notes* to our meeting." Others would walk up to him and remind him to bring certain books, saying, "Mike, remember to bring your *book* to the meeting." At the time of the meeting, Mike had the books but had forgotten his notes.

Your words are very exact and powerful. The brain does not operate on your good intentions; it operates on what you program into it. By this simple example Mike recognized the power of language. Experiment yourself, and soon you will discover that you have probably gotten a lot of what you have actually asked for as opposed to what you wanted. The more you practice, the more simple this will become and the more effective you can be.

You get what you ask for. Make sure you ask for what you really want. Try this out for a while, and you'll notice significant changes in people's responsiveness to you. Some of our customers have actually reported that this change to positives caused others to consider them uplifting, enjoyable people. You are regularly causing them to bring up positive images and memories.

In summary, a key thing to remember is that whatever words you utter must be mentally processed by the other person. You are in control of many of the mental images that they will use while they are listening to you. You are in control of many of the memories which will be recalled whenever they are listening to you. This control, this ability to determine the mental imagery of your prospect or client offers you tremendous potential to powerfully influence them. This is a major feature of your storytelling tool kit. By speaking in positives you are constantly moving toward what you want as opposed to what you don't want. The more you move in the direction of achievement of your goals and desired outcomes, the more you will accomplish them.

Speaking in positives is an extraordinarily powerful communication tool. It's especially helpful when you wish to influence someone's mind toward a particular objective. For example, if you want someone to feel comfortable with you, then you may want to include in your presentation words and phrases that can help you accomplish this objective.

Below is a short list of phrases and sentences which would assist in this process:

Feel better.

I'm sure you'll like this.

This has what you want, right?

Rest assured, our service is excellent.

Perhaps you'll find this interesting, helpful, and informative.

I hope you like it as much as I think you will.

Things are getting better.

I believe this is what you want.

There is more to good positive emphasis than speaking in positives. While this is extremely important, there are other factors for you to know.

How to Kill a Conversation with One Word

The word *but* is one of the most negative words in the English language. Consider a situation in which you are making a point to someone and after you have made your statement he says, "Yes, *but* I think..." You immediately know that he disagrees with you. Even if it isn't true for you, you must realize that the word *but* throws up defensive mechanisms for large numbers of people.

When a person uses *but* in a sentence, it is a signal that what was just said is not acceptable. It gives the impression that the idea was rejected.

But can also be offensive. For example, has anyone ever said to you "Yes, that's a good idea, but listen to this" or "All of those points are fine, but...."? Have you noticed that this tiny three-letter word can have such an impact? Often, using *but* is like letting the person you are talking with believe she has made an impact and then taking it away again. When the word *but* is used, the listener may no longer be listening to anything you have to say. She is probably tuned out, offended, or defending a position.

There Are Better Words to Use

Consider the difference in how you feel when you read the following sentences using *like, and, also,* and *in addition to,* substituted for *but.* Instead of "That's a great idea, but listen to this…"

Try: "That's a great idea, *and* have you thought about…?"

Or, "That's a great idea. *In addition to* that have you thought about…?"

Or, " That's a great idea. Have you also considered…?"

How to Deal with People Who Use *But*

We also should mention the "polarity responder." This is a person who superficially seems negative. The polarity responder is the person who takes exception to almost everything you say. If you say, "It's a lovely day," the polarity responder says, "There are lots of clouds." This person is not necessarily negative. Such a person may seem to be difficult but is merely looking for the exception rather than the rule. The polarity responder usually thinks of himself or herself as hard to fool and realistic. In fact, these individuals are dealing in a useful habitual way, for themselves, with reality.

Think about this: You only have three responses to anything you encounter: positive, negative, or neutral. The polarity responder simply looks for the exception or what could go wrong before he notices the general rule or what is good about something. Unfortunately for this person, he can get into the habit of noticing the exception or what is bad and not the second step and notice what is good.

On the other hand, a Pollyanna will tend to notice only the positive while disregarding the negative. It doesn't take too long before reality gives you a dose of the negative exception to offset overly positive perceptions.

How To Deal with the Polarity Responder

There is a simple, easy way to handle a polarity responder. It resembles the situation in algebra when two negatives cancel each other out and produce a positive. Ordinarily to a positive responder you would say, "I believe you will like this." To a polarity responder you say, "I'm not sure you'll like this." The polarity responder will reply along the lines of "What makes you think so? Of course I'll like it."

If you say, "Don't you want to feel good?" you run the risk of their polarizing. You may try, "You wouldn't want to feel good, would you?" or "You wouldn't want productivity to increase, would you?" or "You probably want to make more money?" Notice the use of negatives, and figure the probable response that the polarity responder will automatically give.

Here is a good example of how effective this can be. Among our clients are two very accomplished men working together as partners. One had decades of experience, and the other, who was much younger, only had about 10 years of experience. Every time the younger man made a suggestion, the older man would respond negatively. We asked the younger man to try negative suggestions such as "You know, partner, I was thinking about this project and I don't think we can pull it off." He felt using this tool was too simple and obvious and could not possibly work. We gave many assurances, so he tried. He called us after the first day of use of the technique and said ecstatically that every single thing he wanted that day he got simply by using negative phrasing. Try it. You'll like it.

The Power of Word Emphasis

The emphasis that we place on words can also affect how our message is received. Despite our best intentions people will sometimes not respond as we expect because they "heard it wrong."

Consider how someone might react to each of the following sentences:

1. *You* look good today.
2. You *look* good today.
3. You look *good* today.
4. You look good *today*.

The first three sentences are usually thought of as complimentary. The last one is heard as an insult. "What do you mean? Don't I look good every day?" You may have meant to give a compliment but accidentally emphasized the wrong word, which changed the entire meaning for the listener. There is an important concept in communication: "The meaning of the communication is the response you get—regardless of your intent." Remember, "What you holler at the mountain is the way your echo comes back (in the form of the other person's reaction to you)."

Let's briefly discuss another common example. In sales, asking the client's opinion is standard operating procedure. Consider the possible client reactions to the question "What do you think?" as different words are emphasized. We've regularly received the following responses when we asked for a group reaction to the word emphasis (not every group member agreed, because of individualized reactions, yet the majority of people agreed with the assessments provided below):

What do you think?

This is generally perceived as a positive request. Upon hearing this, most people find themselves in an information-gathering mode. A few find themselves thinking that they might have to defend themselves.

What *do* you think?

Most people react positively to this question. The consensus is that sincere interest in discovering an opinion was expressed.

What do *you* think?

This question produces an almost universally negative reaction. Comments are along the lines that listeners feel defensive and on-the-spot. Some people picture someone pointing to them and saying, "What did *you* do that for?"

What do you *think?*

This question gets a positive reaction. People feel that the thinking process is being engaged instead of egos.

By emphasizing the you, *the direction goes to the person. By emphasizing* think, *the brain engages in that activity. Emphasis in speaking is like that used by an orchestra conductor, who leads the audience from one emotion to another. Know your objective and use your tools to get you there. You are also like the traffic cop that determines the flow of traffic. Only, you do it with words and style. Things can flow smoothly, or they can be jammed up. You decide. These tools assist you in maintaining control over, and the flow of, your sales presentation.*

What People Hear and What They Remember

Some communication experts, supported by studies, have stated that we hear only about 50 percent of what is said and retain only 10 percent of what we hear; therefore, we hear and retain only 5 percent of what is said. While these figures can vary somewhat, the essential idea remains the same — people only remember a small percentage of the details and tend to remember only the gist of most conversations.

What people remember is partly dependent on their predispositions, partly on their goals during the conversation, and partly on the things that you emphasized by your expressions and/or tonal changes.

Plan which words you want to emphasize. Those are the words that your listener will tend to remember. Even if he doesn't remember the particular words, your client will often remember the emotional response evoked by the words.

Test the Power of Emphasis

Try this experiment on your friends. Write out a discussion on something that you are selling. Read to each of them over the phone the identical script, but change the features, benefits, and advantages that you emphasize with each person. (You might make a few photocopies of the script and then use a highlighter to identify the words and phrases to be emphasized.) After reading the script, ask each friend what he or she remembers. More often than not, your friend's memory will be weighted toward the words you emphasized.

You can also include various positive words and statements to further enhance the effect of your suggestions. While listening to your presentation, the client would also be unconsciously directed to positive associations as indicated earlier in the chapter. The result is a significantly more effective presentation.

In summary, the simple ways of being a more effective sales professional are:

- Speaking in positives.
- Eliminating the word *but*.
- Dealing with the polarity responder.
- Using word emphasis.

You may be very surprised at the impact of these simple tools. As you think about the material from Chap. 8, you'll be able to make additional enhancements to your presentation.

PART 5

Unconscious Processes Related to Sales

You do not change minds at a broad conceptual level. Nor do you change minds "on the average." You change the mind of one person at a time. There is no such thing as the "generic" or "average" person. Each person is an individual and should be treated as such.

You have learned and will continue to learn techniques which allow you to work with the individual. You now have additional flexibility and knowledge that will work anywhere, anytime. This implies that you must have the mental flexibility to respond to the person in front of you and to avoid typecasting.

You have probably had experience with a well-meaning friend who insists that he or she knows what's best for you and tries to push you into something. It could be owning a certain car, a watch with a particular design, or whatever. Usually, our response to this is to feel we are suffering an unwanted imposition.

Customers also react negatively to salespeople who try to impose their own criteria. Insisting that you know what is right for the other person is not selling. It is a mark of the amateur, and it is inadequate as a persuasive approach for changing another person's mind. As with many other situations, asking a lot of questions is the real key to avoiding such a problem.

This part will provide some very interesting information about additional unconscious processes. You will learn how to uncover a person's deepest motivations, how to handle anger and hostility while getting useful information for the sale, and how people actually process information when they make a decision.

As always, these techniques allow you to be more precise in your persuasive communications. Also, as before, you will undoubtedly learn a great deal about yourself.

15
Unconscious, Personal "Hot Buttons"

Suppose we ask you to give us your watch. That's right. We walk up to you out of the blue and say, "I like that watch. Please, will you give it to me?" What would your response be? Most people would say, "No!" and perhaps follow up with a string of expletives about us being presumptuous jerks.

Why would you refuse such a request? In whatever terms you phrase your response, the bottom line is simple: there is no payoff for you. You would be without a watch and would have to spend money to get another. Suppose we start to up the ante by offering a small sum which we know is too little. Gradually, we increase the offer until you cannot refuse. At that moment we have made the point: we have changed your mind from no to yes when we found the specific payoff that satisfied your particular requirements and made our offer worthwhile. In seminars, we often use this example to make a very important point about how the sales professional must create an effective story to get the desired result.

What's in It for Me?

This process of exploring incentives until you hit the right "hot button" is the essence of telling a good story in selling. Eventually everyone will respond to an offer if you are able to identify and satisfy their hot buttons or key criteria. Basically the person asks, "What's in it for me?" This is how the person "scores" for a winning situation. In everyday life, we all have very personal rules that determine whether we decide to buy or not to buy, rules that define a win or a loss. These rules are very important for you to know, because you must satisfy your client's or prospect's key criteria if you hope to make the sale.

When you do not match the customer's criteria and he says no, you have encountered resistance. It means you have not made an offer that met the client's rules for making a yes decision, and the client backs away.

In reality, at least in the reality of most of the superstars, there is no such thing as resistance. There are "hidden agendas," "unspoken concerns," "conflicting ideas," or "misunderstandings." It is at these times that you discover the reason for the objection. You will learn what caused the client to score negatively, which is useful information because the flip side is the client's rule for positive scoring on the same matter. That rule must be satisfied before the sale can be made.

Decision Analysis

Knowing both how your customer makes a decision and what criterion he or she use gives you great sales leverage. Decision analysis is designed to reveal how a person makes a decision.

It is quite useful and is used by successful people on a rather intuitive basis every day. However, it is obvious to some and not to others. Once you know how your customer decides to buy, your presentation will incorporate that knowledge. The example below will give you an idea of how decisions are systematically made.

If you were to interview a job candidate, your opinion of his or her suitability might change as new facts emerged. In this example, a sales candidate is interviewed, and with each item of information the interviewer shifts his opinion. Pretend that you have an opening for a job candidate like the one described below. Would you hire *this* person? Compare your reactions to the way the interviewer reacts to the information as each fact is revealed.

The candidate is rated on scales of 1 to 10 that express the opinion of the interviewer at each step: 1 equals a definite no, 5 equals a 50/50 chance, and 10 equals an absolute yes. As each fact is revealed, the interviewer's changing opinion can be traced by following the path of the boldface numbers.

Fact 1. "He doesn't have direct experience."

1 **2** 3 4 5 6 7 8 9 10

Fact 2. "He sought us out for this interview."

1 2 3 **4** 5 6 7 8 9 10

Fact 3. "He worked his way through college entirely on his own, really loves sales, and has experience in a related field."

1 2 3 4 5 6 **7** 8 9 10

Fact 4. "He has researched the job thoroughly."

1 2 3 4 5 6 7 **8** 9 10

Fact 5: "He seems to have the epilepsy under control with medication since he hasn't had a seizure in 3 years.

1 2 **3** 4 5 6 7 8 9 10

Fact 5. "He set an all-time sales record for the encyclopedia territory and has been living on. that income for the past year.

1 2 3 4 5 6 7 **8** 9 10

Fact 6. "He has drive and discipline."

1 2 3 4 5 6 7 8 9 **10**

In this case the interviewer was generally more impressed as more facts came to light. His decision changed each time more information emerged. He went from a no on fact 1 through progressively improving responses until a final yes (10) as fact 6 was elicited. Of course, in most interviews, opinion will wax and wane on some items as the interviewer has second thoughts. Yet any questionable items might be overridden by some fact that is especially valued by the interviewer. Any half a dozen interviewers will have very different and unique reactions to this same set of facts. Probably your own reactions did not match the judgment of this sample interviewer.

There is at least one very important fact about this way of exploring decision behavior. Each person is unique in how he or she "scores" a situation but also systematic in his or her personal scoring-system methodology. We have found that there is a clear, repeating pattern for each person that can be identified. Each person also has personal reactions to the facts. No two people are alike. This is the way clients in the real world react too.

As you present your story, you want to move the client progressively toward a yes decision. Even though you may miss a point or two, you can override minor missteps when you continually assist the client to achieve a happy ending.

In summary, people make decisions for their own reasons. If you hope to persuade them, you must ask them for information about those reasons. Next, we will discuss how to get this information.

Discovering a Person's Unconscious, Personal "Hot Buttons"

Discovering a client's key criteria or buying motivations allows us to present products in a more effective manner. As already indicated, a crucial aspect of the persuasive process is learning what other people really want and how they decide to get it. Then you are able to more precisely package your offering to help them meet their needs. You will recall a key question to ask is "What do you want in a _____?"

Your Key Decision-Making Criteria

This is an interesting self-evaluation which will demonstrate an important point. It often produces interesting insights into personal behavior. You may also wish to try this with others. Answer the questions below by circling the three or four most appropriate answers to each question:

1. What factors are important to you when deciding to purchase a car?

    1. Good company reputation
    2. Available options for vehicle
    3. Style or looks
    4. Location of dealer
    5. Service available from dealer

    6. Price
    7. Dealer integrity
    8. Dependability
    9. Warranty
    10. Improvements

2. If you were to begin a new career, what would you look for in a company?

    1. Reputation in the field
    2. Multiple career paths
    3. Attractive facility or offices
    4. Location of office
    5. Helpful staff

    6. Money
    7. Company integrity
    8. Reliability
    9. Written contract offered
    10. Company growth record

3. What might influence your choice of a vacation resort?

1. Heard good things about it
2. Many activities available
3. Attractiveness
4. Geographical location
5. Excellent service from staff
6. Cost
7. Honest people
8. Enjoyed yourself there before
9. Assured you will like it
10. New attractions available

4. What do you consider important qualities in a business associate?

1. Reputation
2. Different interests
3. Good appearance
4. Can easily get together
5. Helpful
6. Worthwhile person
7. Honesty
8. Reliability
9. Keeps promises
10. Works at skill development

5. Why do you frequent certain restaurants?

1. Reputation
2. Variety of dishes
3. Atmosphere or ambiance
4. Location
5. Good service
6. Reasonable prices
7. Integrity
8. Consistent quality
9. Satisfaction assured
10. Tries to upgrade food and services

6. What do you pride yourself on (or, what do you admire in someone)?

1. Good reputation
2. Seeks new challenges
3. Provides good image
4. Ease of accessibility
5. Offers assistance
6. Paid for work rendered
7. Trustworthy
8. Reliable
9. Fulfills verbal word
10. Strives for personal excellence

7. Why do you go to a particular clothing store?

1. Excellent reputation
2. Good selection
3. Good looking store
4. Easy to get to
5. Helpful staff
6. Good value for the money
7. Good reputation
8. Quality merchandise
9. Good return policy
10. Keeps up-to-date styles

8. What are some of the qualities you would want in a friend or a spouse?

1. Confidence in the person	6. They're worth the effort
2. Wide range of interests	7. Trustworthy
3. Attractive	8. Dependable
4. Is there when needed	9. His or her word is as good as gold
5. Helpful	10. Pursues self-improvement

1)____ 2)____ 3)____ 4)____ 5)____ 6)____ 7)____ 8)____ 9)____ 10)____

Tabulate the frequency of each number for all answers. For example, if you chose answer 3 in five of the eight questions, its frequency would be five. Most people have a few numbers that receive rather high usage.

Equivalencies

The words associated with each answer number were basically equivalents or synonyms of each other. All the number 1s mean basically the same thing, as do the 2s, etc. Any words or equivalents used on four or more occasions can be considered key criteria or motivational themes for you.

There may be a difference between your responses for the odd-numbered questions and those for the even-numbered questions. The odd-numbered questions are oriented toward things and activities (car, vacation, restaurant, clothing store). The even-numbered questions are oriented toward relationships (company choice, associate, admirable characteristics, friend).

Did you discover certain repeated motivations for yourself? Most people are surprised that they use the same or similar criteria to choose gas stations as they do to choose their friends. This is important information to know about yourself and very important to know about others.

Over 10,000 people have taken variations of these tests, and virtually every one of them had two or three dominant themes running throughout their lives, themes that are important factors in many of their decisions. Knowledge of what these themes are allows you to both more precisely predict someone's response, and present your ideas more persuasively.

There Are More Than Ten Themes

The 10 choices offered to you in the questionnaire above represent only a small portion of the common themes. A more comprehensive list is at the end of this chapter. Unfortunately, there is no single theme that is important to everybody. Each person has his or her own unique set of motivations which you'll be able to discover by asking a series of simple questions — more on this below.

Depending upon the decision your customer is making, certain criteria become the dominant factor. The degree of dominance may vary from one type of decision to another. (An example of this might be purchasing a car versus choosing a restaurant.) *These basic themes in motivation are quite consistent for most individuals.*

This Is What Benefit Selling Is All About

This is the essence that allows benefit selling to occur. Instead of hoping that your client translates generic features and benefits into personally meaningful concepts, you help the process. That is, you tailor your presentation to a particular individual, thus moving away from hit-and-miss, random strategies and toward a fine-tuned strategy which significantly enhances your ability to close the sale. Think about how much more powerful and meaningful your presentations can be by incorporating this information.

When you are making a sale and you have the opportunity to ask your client, "What made you choose *x*?" you will be finding out her criteria. If she tells you why she did not purchase something, she is telling you which criteria were not met, thereby again telling you her criteria.

Key Questions to Ask

Many of the the key questions have already been introduced in this, and earlier, chapters. They are listed again here as both a review and a reference. They would normally be asked in the early phases of your conversation and provide a wealth of information about the client which can include: personal hot buttons, sensory word modes, psychological needs and strategies (which you will learn in Chap. 17). The key questions are:

- "What do you want in a _____?" = Criteria
- "What would having [criteria] do for you?"
- "What features are most important to you?"
- "How will you decide which item to purchase?"
- "What factors will influence your decision?"
- "What are things you like and dislike in the competitor's product?"

The information you obtain from these or similar questions would provide you with the information for the immediate sale. They are especially useful for sales professionals in one-time or limited-number sales situations such as appliances, instruments, and items sold in a store (i.e., the customer comes to you).

However, for those professionals in longer-term, multiple-sale industries such as financial services, health care, etc. (or for those wishing to enhance their personal and professional relationships), additional questions are helpful. When talking to clients in these fields, in which several meetings are customary, you can discover the more consistent themes previously discussed. In a series of three or more casual conversations, or as you get to know someone, you can ask a question such as "I'm looking for a restaurant in your area. What do you recommend and why?" At the next conversation you might ask, "What do you like [dislike] about your job?...car?...computer? ...residence? etc. Keep mental or written notes of their answers and search for consistent themes. Then, fine-tune your presentations. All you must do is know what to listen for, actually listen, and remember to employ the information.

Hot-Button Words and Equivalents

Although people tend to use consistent ways to make decisions, it is rare that someone would repeatedly describe these ways of deciding by using the same words. For example, Betsy may go to a particular gas station because of the large product line, a particular clothing store because of good selection, a restaurant because of variety, and have many things to talk about as a requirement of friendship. In each case, the theme of having multiple options available is dominant. To such a person we would wish to emphasize the concept of multiple choices and use synonyms that indicate choice.

Each row below lists a dominant buying motivation, or hot-button word, followed by synonyms, that occur often in business conversations. Remember that these are rather vague words, which have different meanings to different people.

advertising	reputation	name recognition	familiarity
alternatives	variety	selection	product line
appearance	looks	atmosphere	ambiance
cleanliness	looks	neatness	sanitary
convenience	location	proximity	near
help	service	assistance	support

courtesy	consideration	service	respect
credit	cash flow	bargain	discount
dependability	reliable reputation	confidence	
extras	gifts	incentives	bonuses
habit	tradition	familiarity	sentimental
image	style	status	"in" thing
honor/honest	integrity	honesty	trustworthy
money	price	cost	charge
performance	durability	high standards	holds up
prestige	class	peer pressure	
prompt	quick	speed	
affiliation	relationship	friendship	
quality	value	craftsmanship	
reputation	referral	popularity	
safety	security		
suitability	appropriateness	applicability	
times open	convenience	hours	

16

Handling Anger and Hostility— While Getting Sales Information

It's a foregone conclusion that sooner or later the selling situation will produce a hostile, criticizing, or angry person as a client. That situation may be in a corporate boardroom, a new car showroom, or someone's home. In any case, the gracefulness and personal skill you show under pressure will be one of the key determinants of your sales results.

No matter how good your intentions, if you don't have appropriate techniques to manage hostility, you will not prevail in your effort to persuade. Virtually everyone is phobic in their reactions to criticism and anger that is directed at themselves. We've all been in situations in which someone was critical of us or angry, and for most people it was decidedly uncomfortable. This chapter presents the techniques of fogging and questioning to deal with anger and hostility. These techniques, used singly or in combination, are the basis of an "all-purpose" response to get you out of difficult situations while getting valuable information to use later.

When you are attacked by insult, innuendo, put-down, or other tactic, or if the other person is overly emotional, you can control the situation with the techniques described below. Knowing what to do prevents you from becoming too emotionally entangled in the situation. The basic strategic rationale is it takes two to have an argument or a conflict. This strategic attitude eliminates one of the key ingredients (you) that would have otherwise sustained the conflict. You use an indirect method to control via your dialogue. This method is a form of conversational judo in that it uses the gentle way of managing an attack or disagreement.

The Dynamics of Conflicts

Any conflict has a beginning, a middle, and an end. You know that the attack has some specific purpose—it usually doesn't come from nowhere. The antagonist has a point to make—usually blaming you or your company for something. The person usually has as an ultimate objective—resolution of the problem. And *you* are on the receiving end.

The situation has a defined ending that you can control, and you can change the ending from blame to mutual understanding. When most people are angry or their adrenaline is up for any reason, they do not think clearly—they react emotionally. "Thinking" with one's glands has a very different effect than keeping cool under fire. You will have the advantage if you don't become defensive and do remain in control of yourself. It does not matter if the person is criticizing you, your organization, your service, or anything else, *you can be in control*.

Critics are often not aware of exactly what they want, thereby often falling into the seductive trap of "getting off" on the anger. Yet once the other person feels satisfied at having made his or her point, then the anger process will have ended by putting you back in control. How to manage the process is one of the main points of this chapter.

By the way, a helpful technique is to avoid the word problem *and use* issue *instead. This usually takes part of the bite from the situation. Issue often has significantly less emotionalism attached to it and hence tends to make the discussion more objective. In this way, you can diffuse a difficult, hot situation.*

Part of the task in using the techniques described below is to generate an unexpected source of satisfaction for the other person. Part of this source of satisfaction is that you will be attentively listening to the criticism, which from the other person's perspective, is justifiable. In many situations, if you were in his shoes—with the information he has—you would probably feel the same way. Always ask yourself, "What perspective did he have to have in order to feel this way?" This is especially true if he seems to be attacking you as a person rather than as the representative of a company.

Most people don't know you well enough to attack you personally. Even then, it's usually a particular behavior or situation that they are responding to. One of the best responses to criticism is "to become curious, not furious." This way, your curiosity as to how they got that response will lead you to gather information from the other person, rather than to try to defend yourself. With this attitude you become part of the solution.

Throughout this chapter you will be learning techniques to manage this process. However, your attitude is a major factor. Always try to "walk in the other person's shoes," and you'll be able to handle anything. Furthermore, your effort will be much appreciated.

Fogging—Interrupting the Ritual

If you have observed many arguments, you will notice that there is almost a ritualistic aspect to them. One person attacks, the other person defends. Counterattack, defend. Back and forth they go until one person is decided the winner or both walk away angry. In either situation, they both lose. You, however, can maneuver the situation in a way that is different than the usual defensive mode, thereby gaining the advantage. When you don't defend, you break the ritual that people expect.

When you interrupt the ritual, the person usually doesn't quite know what to do and will unconsciously follow any lead that you provide. You provide relief and closure by asking a question that indicates you want to understand rather than to argue which leads to an entirely different approach—the argument becomes an information exchange with mutual cooperation. This alternative response of being very understanding allows you to return to your original goal in the dialogue once you have completed the technique and disarmed the other person's attack. In addition, you certainly don't want a critic to score at your expense. To get a win-win outcome, you must manage the events.

The source of the term *fogging* is in a child's pastime that most people would remember. You are trying to throw rocks at a target, and you can gauge your success by noticing how close you come to actually hitting the target. However, how long would you play if a thick fog totally hid the target? One or two more throws perhaps, and then you would just quit. "It's no fun anymore," you would probably say. Similarly the fogging technique causes a conversational fog to roll in, thereby removing you as the target.

How It Works

Before outlining steps of the technique, here is an example which should give you the basic flavor of the exchange:

> CLIENT: (*angrily*) You people are giving me bad service, and I want it changed.
>
> YOU: I can understand that you are upset. Exactly what would you want done that would allow you to feel okay?
>
> CLIENT: (*still angry*) If the problem were taken care of when promised, I wouldn't be so angry.
>
> YOU: So, if the issue were taken care of on time you'd feel better? What else would need to be done?
>
> CLIENT: The service reps also need to be more courteous. They don't seem to care.
>
> YOU: Then, if they got the job done on time and were more courteous, the issue would be resolved?
>
> CLIENT: Yes. (*substantially cooled off*)

It is important to note from the above exchange that *nothing has been agreed to* thus far. The client has merely cooled off, and we know that promptness and courtesy are critical factors for him. At this point it would be impossible to ensure that the service department would fulfill its end of the bargain because they have not yet been consulted or even told about the issue. Furthermore, we still need to discover exactly what was meant by "service" and "promptness."

The net effect is that the anger has been neutralized and we have obtained information that will be important to this relationship. We can now continue with the dialogue in a more effective way and create a win-win situation.

Additional Initial Responses

Here are some additional initial responses that will lead to the effective use of the fogging technique.

- "Well, I can see you are upset. Tell me what will provide what you need."
- "It is obvious you really mean that. How could it have been done differently?"
- "I think I understand. What specific things will improve the situation?"

Review

First you acknowledge the person's comment, and then you question toward a desired outcome. Your question amounts to "How will you and I know when you have made your point?" Then you follow it by asking for his or her definition of a solution, getting as much information as possible. Then you have a goal to share. You actually help the person make the point regarding the complaint or concern. This is an unusual move, because his or her expectations of an argument are deflected or bypassed. This technique helps bring passions under control and replaces emotion with disciplined thought. That is, the person moves out of his or her emotional mode into an intellectual, fact-finding mode. Many people think this is too simple an idea to work. Believe in it! It works and works well.

How to Fend Off a Personal Attack

The sample dialogue illustrated one type of argument. Yet, a typical interaction would likely sound a bit more like this short dialogue, where the pattern of fog-question prevents defensiveness. Here, George is smugly insulting to Harry. Notice how Harry leads George's responses at each step.

> GEORGE: I think your promotion to management was premature.
>
> HARRY: I suppose you could be right. [Which also states that George could be wrong.] What would you suggest that I do to improve things?
>
> GEORGE: Obviously, you don't know how to manage. You should learn how to do it.
>
> HARRY: I see. And what would let you know if I were to do it more effectively?
>
> GEORGE: You would do things and think more like me.
>
> HARRY: You seem quite certain. Can you give me specific examples?

In this example, Harry avoids criticism, argumentativeness, competition, dominance, or put-downs, even though George may richly deserve a rap on the knuckles. You neutralize power games with this approach. As a result, you have more power, since you are in control.

The value of neutralizing the power games is similar to that of taking the static out of a telephone line—it makes it possible to hear what is going on so you can respond to your advantage. Additionally, you get important information about the person that will ultimately tell you how to win that person over to your way of thinking. In this situation Harry would have found out exactly what George needed to see. How Harry uses the information is another issue. The fogging technique, has given Harry invaluable information regarding George while simultaneously diffusing anger and hostility.

You are changing a free-for-all into something resembling the game plan of a sporting event. You are setting up a plan of dialogue that has a framework similar to that of any major sport such as football, baseball, or basketball. The analogy to sports is accurate in that you define the moves that the other person can make in the discussion, and you define when points are scored and when a win is declared, all in a positive, win-win framework. Also, your control is very indirect and subtle.

If you have ever witnessed someone on the losing end of an argument, you may have noticed that the loser resented it and got even at the first opportunity. No one wins an argument, but persuasion always wins when you have the tools. There are many aspects to persuasion, as this book illustrates. For example, you have learned how language and questions direct the mind. Direct your questions in positives, and try to gather information.

"Keep it simple" is the key to this technique. The essence of the approach is to limit the hassle, control the situation, and put the burden of getting out of the upset state on the other person...with a little help from you.

How to Try the Technique on Others

It would be wise if your practiced this technique with some friends. If the last time someone criticized you, you reacted with anything more than calm curiosity, you should strongly consider practicing this technique in a riskless environment; most people are "criticism-phobic" and need practice before this technique becomes an automatic response. (In Chap. 24 you will learn how to mentally program yourself for ideal reactions.)

Do a practice session or two with a friend in which he pretends to criticize and yell at you. Follow the steps of the technique, and question him about his concerns. Also refer to the skills of verbal pacing and leading in Chap. 11. It is important to also practice matching the tone and/or intensity of his speech pattern initially and then lead him to a tone more conducive to rational discussion. Remember the formula:

Fog: Agree or acknowledge that the person is concerned.

Question: Ask, what specifically would you like?

Verify: Periodically restate the person's comments.

Practice our responses to some typical comments:

- *I think your clothes are atrocious.*   I'm always willing to listen to advice. What would you recommend?
- *What's wrong with your stupid company?*   Obviously you are upset. What has happened?
- *Your sales technique is the pits.*   Since you have noticed what I have been doing, would you tell me what would work more effectively?

From here on, try it without our hints. Also, it would probably be useful to include any comments that you regularly hear or are fearful of hearing. You'll notice that some of them are in an objectionlike format. The technique works just as well.

- Your company is always late on the market.
- The price is too high.
- My boss will never buy this idea.
- Will you just shut up and listen to me?
- Where did you get that stupid suit?
- You'll just have to give us a bigger discount.
- I prefer the competition over your company.
- Come back next year.
- We don't have the budget.
- Your product is not competitive.
- The other salesman gave me a case of wine.
- I could help you get the order with a little incentive.
- Your features just aren't current with the market.
- I don't see any payoff in this.
- Were your program designers drunk?
- You never deliver what you promise.
- I stuck my neck out for you, and you blew it.

Some of these require some thought before you formulate a response. Now is the time to practice, not when it really counts.

How to Gather Additional Information and Retain Control

All you need do in essence to make the game plan work is (1) to respond agreeably no matter what the provocation is and (2) to ask leading questions along a certain line of logic. The pointers to keep in mind are continue to gather information about what the other person needs in order to feel better and use verbs in the present and future tenses because that keeps the dialogue going forward to a new outcome rather than stuck in the past, haggling over what went wrong. Here is an example: "Your need for prompt, courteous service is something that we will make sure is addressed. There are a few additional things that I would also like to discuss with you regarding your future needs."

If a salesperson defines the sales interview as a contest with the client, the salesperson will lose, since no one ever wins an argument. If a customer criticizes you or the item you are presenting, you can use this all-purpose and foolproof way to turn things around and lead the customer to a state of mind that will pay off with a win-win outcome. This was the basic technique used by Benjamin Franklin and the legendary philosopher, Socrates.

The interactions between people seem to work best when emotions are positive. The goal is to avoid eliciting negative emotional responses in the dialogue and to get a neutral or positive response instead. The judolike, fogging technique is used to create the opportunity to follow with questions.

Questioning

Questioning works via a different mechanism than does fogging; questioning causes the equivalent of a mental vacuum in the other person's mind. Physics teaches that air rushes in to fill a vacuum. A question creates a mental vacuum that is instantly filled with images that represent the person's answer. Can you not think of a pink elephant? You have no choice. Your mind responds. Each response to a question provides you with the opportunity to get even more precise information in the form of needs and desires. As long as the person is answering your questions, you have control.

Leading questions, as an extension of the technique, are based on the assumption that you know where you want the dialogue to go. In this context it means that you will arrange your questions to move the person step by step through a few items of information until he or she arrives at the conclusion you have in mind.

Another Great Technique from Benjamin Franklin

You know the power a question has on the mind. Let's examine how that technique of fogging combines very nicely with questioning in the way described to us in the autobiography of Benjamin Franklin.

Franklin's autobiography gives us the origin of the fogging and questioning techniques. He was a vigorous debater and writes that he usually won his arguments — with the result that he created intensely negative feelings on the part of his defeated opponents. Franklin was thought of as brilliant but insensitive, opinionated, and egotistical due to his I-win-you-lose approach. He initially saw persuasion as a competitive win-lose contest with an opponent instead of a situation calling for mutual gain. Franklin debated and argued, but he eventually learned that no one ever wins an argument. Resentments flare and resistance goes underground to haunt the winner.

One day a helpful friend took him aside and showed Franklin a way to win his points and leave the opponent with positive feelings. He learned that when the other person states an opinion, he (Franklin) should acknowledge the statement or agree in principle (not in substance, or with the content of the opinion) that indeed the other person has an opinion. Then ask a question about when, why, where, or how the person formed that opinion. Then use his next response and the next to lead him piecemeal to your goal.

The agreeable recognition of the other person's opinion does not implicitly criticize the person. By then asking a question, new information is acquired. Step by step and question by question, you lead the other person to the conclusion you want him or her to discover. After a few exchanges of this type, you will change the mind of the other person.

As Benjamin Franklin said, explaining a variant of the above procedure: "The best way to convince another is to state your case moderately and accurately. Then say, of course you may be mistaken about it; which causes your listener to receive what you have to say and, like as not, turn about and convince you of it, since you are in doubt."

The Socratic Approach

Socrates had a variant of this method for persuading people to his point of view. It is fully documented that he was an extraordinarily persuasive individual. His method is the essence of simplicity and is a forerunner of Franklin's method. When Socrates wanted to change someone's mind, he would ask them a question, observe the response he obtained, and use the response to form the next question to lead them step by step to the result he wanted.

Socrates didn't argue in the usual sense of raised voices and insistence about who is right and who is wrong. He didn't need to argue, because he was always in control and was generally agreeable. He knew he could control anyone's thinking with a question.

The Dark Room

The relevance of questioning can be summarized through the "dark room" metaphor. Suppose you were to wake up in a totally dark place with no idea of where you were? Like most people you would get up very slowly, carefully feeling your way around until you located a light switch or a door. Otherwise, there is no telling what you might bump into or fall over. Every dialogue is like a dark room at first. Therefore, it is presumptuous and risky to assume you know what is on the other person's mind. Until you realize what is on the other person's mind, you are in that dark room and should ask exploratory questions to shed some light on the subject. Of course the most important questions define the client's situation and his or her version of a happy ending.

How to Change a Mind with Questions

Now let's see how Socrates might use his approach to sell his client, Nick, on a new item of word processing software and computer keyboard. The new software and keyboard will compute customer discounts automatically, saving the user the task of hand calculation, which is time-consuming and awkward.

Nick hates to work with numbers but has argued against the change because he is worried that the new feature would be too hard to learn.

Socrates illustrates how easy and user-friendly the change can be. Notice especially how Socrates uses a clever selling method, as they sit at the word processor together. He builds a series of yes responses and allows the client to come to the desired conclusion.

> SOCRATES: Do you notice, the keyboard has a separate set of keys to enter numerical information?
>
> NICK: Yes, they are just off to the side of the regular keyboard.

SOCRATES: Does a move of your wrist easily position your hand over the numerical keyboard?

NICK: Yes, it does.

SOCRATES: Would you please touch the key marked "calculate" and enter this set of sample figures I'm handing you now?

NICK: Okay, here goes. (*enters the numbers*)

SOCRATES: Now that they are entered, would you touch the key marked "enter" and tell me what happens?

NICK: Okay. (*pause*) Oh, wow! It enters the figures in just the right place in the letter, and the discount is already calculated.

SOCRATES: Does this eliminate several steps in getting answers?

NICK: Yes, it sure does.

SOCRATES: Is it easier to do the work this way?

NICK: Yes, it is.

SOCRATES: Do you prefer this new way over the old way?

NICK: Yes, of course. This is easy.

Question, Observe, Utilize, Question: The QUOQ Model

Now let's analyze this simple dialogue to find out how powerful it really is. You will notice that Socrates *questioned* Nick to identify his attitude or position on the subject at hand. Then Socrates *observed* the client's reaction and *utilized* that reaction to ask his next leading *question*. In sales it is very useful to ask leading questions (even if it is not allowed in courtrooms).

Also you would be accurate to characterize the client's initial state of mind as uninformed. Initially, Nick did not know what was "good" for him. Socrates informed him of some new information, and it was enough to change his mind. This was partly because Socrates met Nick's criteria for simplicity and ease, as well as the need for a convincing demonstration. In other words, while the new situation was better for the client, he did not realize it yet. This is often the case in selling situations.

Naturally, you would characterize the client's end state of mind as informed and changed. That is, the client learned something in the dialogue and changed his mind.

Also it is worth noting that Socrates questioned the client into agreeing with his own conclusion. He did not argue or insist on his own point of view. He found out what would convince Nick by asking first. He did no guessing or mind reading. In this case, Nick needed the calculator to be both simple and easy to learn. Socrates then asked questions that would lead to that conclusion.

This is an example of a subtle change of mind that will affect clients' behavior directly. Nick bought the idea because it was presented to him in a way that was irresistible to him. The approach created a new and different feeling regarding something he had resisted until then.

Socrates avoided any argument or criticism. Yet, Socrates did have a planned, hidden agenda of how he was going to proceed. He was quite deliberate. Intuition was not a large factor here. Relying on intuition can be dangerous if it is not backed up by deliberate know-how. You might ask yourself Did Socrates sell or tell Nick? Obviously, he sold him. He did not tell him what he "ought" to do. He convincingly "sold" him with the technique. You would also have to characterize Socrates' strategy as indirect and persuasive rather than direct or argumentative.

Important Rules of the Game

Think about it from a slightly different perspective. Where do sales interviews, meetings, and presentations tend to fall apart? When disagreement over opinions turns to argument and conflict. You can't communicate on the phone if there is static. Similarly, negative emotions are the kind of static that stops human communication. How does the individual avoid disagreement? There are several facets to the answer:

1. Set up your attitude and opening remarks to prevent competitive or argumentative tones and postures, i.e., "fighting words" as the pioneers used to call them, for example, "My job is to help you get the product most appropriate for your needs."

2. Don't inadvertently try to score points at the other person's expense. You might win an argument, but you will lose the sale. Assume that the customer is always right. You might want to follow the Golden Rule: "He or she who has the gold makes the rules." The customer ultimately is the final arbiter because of the power of the purse. Never alienate the person who has the gold, no matter how good you think it may feel.

3. Try to score for a mutual payoff with the courteous attitude: "How can I help you?" Your sale should genuinely help the customer. Your job is to show her how in terms that she will like and find convincing.

4. Use fogging and questioning to lead the dialogue in useful directions. It is virtually impossible to have a negative outcome when you control the direction of the dialogue with these techniques. In addi-

tion to being useful tools for disarming hostility, they have the virtue of being the same tools to use to find out what the customer wants and what his rules are for deciding to buy. You simply use questions to find out what these rules are.

5. The power of these techniques means you need never feel defensive. The essence of the fogging-questioning pattern is acknowledge the criticism in principle, *not* in content. Then ask a leading question, for example, "I notice you feel quite certain. How did you come to that conclusion?" or "What consequences will it have?" or "What if x and y and z were part of the consideration, how might you change your thinking?" Always ask about who, what, where, when, why, and how, as the context dictates your purpose. Focusing toward the future also keeps the objective pointed toward what can be done once agreement is reached.

We often find that there are additional things which are not expressed when the first question is asked. Therefore, be prepared to further explore the client's response by asking "What else would make a difference?" Ultimately, you will get all of the client's key concerns and criteria, which you can then use in your sales presentation—now or sometime in the future.

17
Strategies

Strategies are one of the most significant tools in the world of selling. Strategies are specific and identifiable behavioral sequences that have a predictable effect. In some situations you might prefer to call strategies the essence of a person's style. Strategies add to your ability to actually know what goes on inside the person, and when combined with your other tools, allow you to tell a virtually irresistible story.

Mental Rules

Strategies amount to predictable patterns of behavior which you can use to manage a selling situation. They are the invisible mental rules customers use when deciding to buy something. Anything in human behavior that repeats itself becomes predictable. You can use this predictability for your mutual benefit. Here are a few simple repeating behaviors.

You have a strategy for evaluating new ideas, another for choosing the clothes you will wear, another for ordering lunch, and still another for getting motivated. Each of these repeating patterns works consistently from one day to the next. They become mental grooves. The way we decide to buy something also is a repeating behavior. The key to finding that repeating behavior is located in the ways people express themselves, in their use of language.

The use of strategies to more effectively influence someone is illustrated by Jerry. Jerry was appearing in court to present his case to a judge for a minor traffic offense. Jerry arrived early and sat in on some cases that were on the docket before his. For one case the judge said, "As I *look* at the evidence of this case I can't help but *feel* that there is something missing. After *listening* to the testimony, I find that I am

167

unconvinced that the speeding ticket was given in error." For another case the judge said, "The evidence clearly *shows* that the accident was unavoidable, and I *feel comfortable* that everything was examined from all angles. After *hearing* the testimony of the parties involved, I must dismiss the charge of reckless driving."

Jerry realized that the judge was following a particular thinking sequence in which something had to create a mentally complete picture which would result in the judge having a feeling or gut response. Then, verbal testimony would either confirm or conflict with the documentation. The summarized sequence was visual to kinesthetic to auditory. That sequence was the system of rules, the strategy, the judge used to decide.

When Jerry pleaded his case he said: "Your Honor, I'm sure that as you *look* at the evidence that I am providing you will definitely *see* that I was acting correctly. I'm also sure that you would have *reacted* in a similar way and will *feel* that my actions were correct. I'll also *describe* the situation fully so that you can *feel* comfortable that any *questions* you may have are fully *answered*." The judge ruled in Jerry's favor. Jerry made his case more palatable, reasonable, logical, and convincing because it was presented in the judge's habitual thinking sequence.

How to Read a Customer's Strategy

Let's illustrate how a strategy works in a customer. Suppose you are selling new cars, and an individual is looking at the cars in the showroom. You ask, "How can I help you?" The customer responds, "I'd like a nice new car." At this point you know in general terms what he wants. But your information needs to be more specific to get anywhere. You might ask, "What features in particular are most important to you?" Let's suppose he responds, "Sleek styling, sports car handling, and fuel economy."

Those three items (styling, handling, economy) are his criteria words and mean you are *not* going to emphasize luxury packages and jack rabbit starts. So far he has told you in his criteria words, how he "scores" for a winner of a car.

You also need to know how he decides, as he plays the game of being a buyer. The judge told Jerry how he decided by his behavior and words. But you don't have Jerry's opportunity to spend a lot of time watching a customer. To shorten the time to learn the customer's strategy you ask a question.

Just Ask

You ask, straightforwardly, "How will you decide which car is the one for you to buy?" (This is a more considerate version of the rather blunt question "What does it take to sell you this car?")

At this point you want to watch his eyes and his body language, as well as listen carefully to what he says. Even if he is being shrewd and refuses to give you a straight answer, he will answer the question in his own mind. As he answers in his own mind, his eyes will cycle through a specific pattern. This is the indicator of his decision strategy. He will be doing what the judge did with his decisions, but the strategy is compressed into a moment or two of thought on the customer's part.

That pattern is the answer you need. You can identify it by watching his eyes and his words. His answer might be "I want sleek styling, sports car handling, and fuel economy." As he tells you this, suppose he looks up and to his left [⊙⊙] , then horizontally to his right [⊙⊙] and then down and to his right [⊙⊙] . You would then know that he has three steps to his decision-making strategy: he sees an image, he hears something, and he has a feeling. It doesn't matter to you exactly what he sees, hears, and feels in his mind; it is enough for you to know the pattern from the outside.

The number of steps in a strategy varies from person to person, but seldom are there more than a few. The words the person uses will usually echo that eye pattern. Even if you have a bit of trouble the first time, you have another chance; the customer will repeat his or her pattern in the conversation again.

Let's continue with the example begun above. After you notice the customer's pattern, you then repeat this pattern back to him in your subsequent dialogue. You state the same combination that he indicated in his response. He has told you that he decides by *seeing* (visual) something like the style or color, *hearing* (auditory) something like the solid clunk of the door or the radio, and knowing how good he will *feel* (kinesthetic) by having this economical car. In plain English, you'd say something such as, "Well, Mr. Jones, as you *look* at the style of this car and notice the quality *sound* of this car's engine you can *feel* sure that it will be as economical as you expect."

You have echoed his decision-making strategy of seeing, hearing, and feeling even though he wasn't aware that he expressed it to you in his words and eye patterns. And to top it off you have also combined it with two of his three criteria words, style and economy. Since you will likely have a few minutes with the customer, you will be able to use all three of his criteria words in other comments you make as the conversation progresses.

What If You Don't Have the Exact Item?

Based on his original answer, the customer seems to be describing a small sports car. But for the sake of illustration, let's suppose you only sell midsize cars. Superficially, that may seem like a very big problem. How do you sell a midsize car to someone who is describing what sounds to you like the opposite? You describe your offering in terms of the customer's strategy. So let's replay the idea so that the midsize seems more like a sportier model while using the same pattern with slightly different words.

You could say, "Well, sir, did you see the sleek lines of the car that is on display? The sticker says that it gets excellent mileage. The handling is very much in the sports car class." You have echoed his strategy and his criteria words. This sort of move is calculated to engage the customer's mind by echoing the customer's own logic. It works.

The above suggestion is made on the assumption that what you have is appropriate for the client. Don't fall into the trap of pushing something down someone's throat. Remember to use fogging and questioning techniques, and seek information from customers' buying motivations to make a more informed decision.

If what you have is appropriate, by all means try to sell it to the client. However, if the client has needs, wants, and desires that you cannot fulfill, you are better off referring him or her elsewhere.

As mentioned throughout, there are ethical considerations. Remember, to have a happy ending to the story both you and the client must be winners.

Matching the customer's criteria words and verbal and eye sequences allows you to significantly increase the persuasive power of your story. The eye pattern and verbal word choice may not always be closely correlated, but usually they are. When in doubt, use the sequence of the eyes.

For instance, assume that a customer made the following statement, "Let me take a *look* at the literature. That will give me a *sense* of what you're offering. Then, after a *demonstration*, I'll *ask you to clear up* any questions that I may have." Which of the following would be the best approach for the salesperson to take, since the customer is indicating a four-step look-feel-do-ask sequence?

1. Tell the customer about the item and offer the literature only after the presentation is made?

2. Provide a demonstration, ask questions, and then provide literature?

3. Provide literature, give the demonstration, and then respond to questions?

The last option most closely matches the approach requested by the customer. We intuitively know that the customer's request must be attended to in some manner. We may merely hand her the printed information and barely give her a chance to look at it before beginning a demonstration or a verbal presentation. We may suggest an alternative approach. In either case, the customer has described her strategy, and we should try to follow that sequence.

When we consider the possible consequences of not following the client's lead, it seems obvious that we should comply with the client's wishes. As a professional communicator you know that most sales are made or lost depending on how comfortable the client is with you. If you can make the client comfortable and pleased by respecting his or her wishes, you are better off. Unfortunately, there are many people who follow their own agendas regardless of customers' needs. They are usually relegated to sales mediocrity.

Discovering a customer's strategy is of tremendous benefit for anyone involved in sales. A sales presentation of any idea can be presented in a way that replicates the way the person normally makes a decision — greatly increasing the probability of acceptance.

As much as possible match the client's unique strategy. Trial and error is not acceptable, since you have so much at stake. The way to accurately "map" the customer's behavior is to use the following tools:

- A good leading question that reveals his or her patterns
- The skill to watch the response for eye pattern sequence
- The skill to listen for key words
- The skill to echo those items to the client in your response

Your Own Strategies

Everyone has had occasions of peak performance. In those moments we were able to accomplish our tasks easily and effectively. We have also experienced days in which we couldn't seem to get out of our own way.

The difference between the two states of mind, assuming no medical problem, is often the use of efficient or inefficient thinking sequences, i.e., strategies.

This "off-day" behavior has its roots below the conscious level of awareness. This makes it extremely difficult to understand what's wrong at the time. Normally, we have to wait until we naturally cycle back to our normal self.

You could, however, override the off-day behavior if your peak performance strategy had been previously identified. Then, whenever you had an off day, you would be able to reengage your full horsepower yourself by consciously triggering your own peak performance sequence.

One of our clients is a marathon runner who occasionally failed to mentally rehearse the first few steps which mentally "got her going." At those times, she performed poorly in the run. Her strategy for peak performance was identified and used to teach her how to put herself in the best mental frame possible. Now, whenever she doesn't feel just right before a race, she knows to mentally rehearse. She is now much more consistent in her performances. Differences like these can and do make all the difference in the world. (Part 7, "Empower Yourself for Sales Success," will provide help in this matter.)

This "fix-it" technique can be applied to many types of situations— from mental to physical proficiency. However, it takes a qualified coach to work you through the process. You can't do this yourself any more than a brain surgeon could perform surgery on herself. This tool becomes important when you realize that all of us have a strategy for everything we do. All behavior is connected to strategies.

PART 6

Getting the Order and Following Up

Everything thus far has been designed to ensure sales success. You have learned quite a few things about conscious and unconscious processes. As you employ these techniques, your level of efficiency should start to soar.

When you think about it, all of the information you have learned and all of the techniques you've gained have been designed to bring you to the closing. You should be obtaining a very high closing rate with your clients because, given the structure of the techniques, it should be irrational for the client to say anything other than yes.

No matter how perfect your presentation or how strong your close, there will be people who have last-minute doubts, hesitations, and concerns. This is to be both expected and happily anticipated because they are giving you even more valuable information which you'll then incorporate into the close. "The sale begins when the client says no" is a very true saying. In this part, you'll learn to work with people to help them deal with their issues.

Sometimes sales are lost because the salesperson makes a mistake. You'll receive some self-evaluation materials to help you pinpoint areas that need further development. Even with this knowledge, some people may still not be able to close the sale, and the causes for their poor performance must be identified. Occasionally it is the economy, the market, the product line, or other uncontrollable outside factors. Most of the time, however, it is personal, internal factors which must be addressed. The "How To, Want To, Chance To" analysis will assist here. (The final part of the book, Part 7, will deal with mentally conditioning yourself for sales success. More on that at the appropriate time.) In this part you will learn techniques for:

Getting the order

Using client objections or hesitancy to your advantage

Getting referrals

Achieving account penetration

You'll find that many of the concepts have already been introduced in previous chapters, allowing us to be brief. As always, you'll be able to use this knowledge immediately.

18
Getting the Order

In a sense, every aspect of your discussion with your prospect or client has been a prelude to the close. From the initial meeting where you established rapport, to the discussions and questions determining needs and motivations, and through the presentation—all was designed to get the order.

Closing the sale should be the logical conclusion of everything that has previously occurred. You have been working on what is now popularly called the "consultative" selling approach, where you view people like family members and friends rather than like dollar signs. As a result, there is little or no need to push the person. Instead, you lead the person to the appropriate conclusion. It creates a positive, win-win situation which is helpful for referrals and repeat business.

Sometimes You Just Gotta Ask

The biggest problem that people have in closing is actually asking for the order. Many sales people avoid it like the plague even though it is their primary purpose. It is important to realize that most clients will not ask to place the order themselves. Psychologically, it is easier for clients to say yes to you than to ask you to take their order. Furthermore, most people fear change (even though it may be positive) and must be motivated to actually get off the fence and make a decision. It is a primary part of your job to help them in that process. Otherwise, everything thus far will have been a waste of time and your career will be dependent on pure luck. As the adage says, "Luck is given and luck is taken away. Luck is the least sure of all events."

Why Salespeople Don't Ask for the Order

Salespeople avoid asking for the order for many reasons, including the belief that people neither can, nor should, be influenced; the potential for displeasing the client; the rejection that may result from asking ("If I don't ask, he may not buy, but he won't reject me"); or the bogeyman will get them.

That last fear is as ridiculous as any other. If you laughed at it, then also laugh at any other fear that you or others may have. Always ask yourself, "What is the absolutely worst thing that can happen if I ask for the order?" The client is not going to throw eggs at you, you won't be thrown out on your ear, and no one will laugh at you. The very worst that can happen is that the person says no, and then you have the opportunity to find out why. When you find out the reason or reasons, you are also discovering key motivations, which can then be addressed. This will be covered in Chap. 19.

Of course, the other side of the coin is that you can choose not to ask for the order and be relegated to sales mediocrity or, using a euphemism from modern business, eventually terminated. The unfortunate part is that some people will allow themselves to be fired rather than put their egos on the line. Again, there are ways of dealing with this mental issue, which are addressed in Part 7.

A Purchase Should Be the Next Logical Step

The client's purchase of your product or service should be the logical conclusion of your discussion. This is accomplished by carefully reviewing the benefits to be received and making sure that the client agrees that the product or service will fulfill a particular need. It is basically the review of the happy ending.

You already know what the client wants in the product. You also know what it will do for him or her. Then, it is a matter of reminding the client that you have the solution.

Closing Techniques

The following review provides the essential ideas needed to effectively close the sale.

- Review the client's key objective or need.
- Summarize accepted features, benefits, and advantages.
- Indicate how the product or service will accomplish that objective.
- Ask for the order.

There are stylistic differences in how you present the summary as well as in how you ask for the order. The summary should be coordinated to the approach you had taken in the sales presentation. That is, if you were using visual aids, continue to do so. The idea is to have a smooth transition from the presentation segment to the closing segment.

Some popular techniques are presented here as a brief review. They all are effective at different times. However, no one technique works with everyone. It is often easy to determine which to use because your client will have given you many preliminary indications in your previous discussions.

The Ben Franklin–Balance Sheet Close

Here you take a piece of paper and compare the advantages listed on one side to the disadvantages listed on the other. (Remember to provide the client with ample opportunity to list any disadvantages from her perspective. It's better to have these listed up front, than to have them hidden and unstated.)

This is most effective on those people who have previously asked you to compare and contrast. Often they'll say something like "How do these things compare?" or "How do they stack up?" The Ben Franklin approach will match the client's preferred thought process.

The Either-Or Close

A comparison between two attractive alternatives is the basis of this technique. Here you want the client to purchase either product A or product B. Each one is equally good. You compare one to the other and allow the client to choose. "Do you want the red car or the green car" is the essential choice. The client is already sold.

This is obvious when the person continually asks for a comparison between one item and the next. It can be used as the final aspect of the Franklin close.

The Assumptive Close

You assume a client has already positively decided and now work on the details of the transaction. Occasionally, a person gets so caught up doing the paperwork that they don't consciously appreciate that they have made the purchase.

The Limited-Supply Close

This is appropriate when there is actually a limited supply of your product. However, you run the risk that the client will feel pushed, and this close has been used so often that it may cause the client to doubt your credibility.

The We're-In-This-Together Close

Some people are afraid to make a decision by themselves. They indicate this by questions like, "So, what do you think?" or "Where do we go from here?" or other items which show that you are a part of the team. If this is the case, you would also want to indicate that you have a vested interest in the client's well-being and then to use words such as "we," "let's," "us," and "together."

The You-Owe-It-to-Yourself Close

Any benefits for the individual or the family that can be imagined can be stated as part of your close. Consequently, if in your previous conversation the person said, "I deserve something like this," then this close would have added persuasive power. A comment like, "This is something you deserve" (echoing the client's words), or "You owe it to yourself" (more subtly echoing the client's words) will probably have impact.

Of course, you could have the client again recall the happy ending, and you will have basically accomplished the same purpose. A minor modification would take care of the person who indicated how others would be benefited.

The Authority Close

Many people need to have the decision made for them. Throughout their lives friends and family members have told them what to do. "What would you do if you were me?" is a common question for such people. "What should I do?" is another cry for an authority figure — you — to step in and assist them in their moment of need.

The Best Close

We'll end the same way we began this closing section: "There's no way around it. Sometimes you just gotta ask for the order."

If I were you, I would literally keep track of the number of times I made full or partial presentations, and the number of times I actually asked for the order. Your sales will increase dramatically the moment you pay conscious attention to asking for the order. Most people are amazed at how rarely they say something like, "I'd like to place an order for this car...this machine...this policy...this whatever."

No wishy-washy, "sorta-kinda" stuff — go for it! Ask for the order! If you do that, you will win with regularity. If you don't do it, you've wasted your time and energy. Go back and review close 6, above. How does what I've just said apply to you? To a large extent, your answer will determine your success level.

Sales Evaluation Sheet

Here is an evaluation sheet which may help you in evaluating your sales calls. Whether you make the sale or not, always ask yourself what you could be doing even better. This will help ensure your long-term success. It is only through constant evaluation that you can rise to the ranks of stardom.

Sales Evaluation Sheet

Getting Attention

Stated the reason for the call	_____ Yes	_____ No
Offered a benefit	_____ Yes	_____ No

One way I can improve:_____

Handling Indifference

Asked closed probes to uncover specific needs or dissatisfactions	_____ Yes	_____ No
Asked open probes to get the suspect to begin talking	_____ Yes	_____ No

One way I can improve:_____

Qualifying the Prospect or Client

Qualified in terms of budget	_____ Yes	_____ No
Qualified in terms of objectives	_____ Yes	_____ No
Qualified in terms of attitude	_____ Yes	_____ No

One way I can improve:_____

Gaining Commitment

Appealed to a need	_____ Yes	_____ No
Offered benefits	_____ Yes	_____ No
Asked for a specific commitment	_____ Yes	_____ No

One way I can improve:_____

As mentioned earlier, regardless of how excellent your presentation is, and how powerful your close, you will regularly encounter client stalls and objections — the subject of Chap. 19.

19
Client Hesitancy and Objections

If selling were merely asking for the order and getting it, you would not have any potential for additional commissions. You, and everyone else in sales, would be on a fixed salary. Selling may be one of the highest paying professions but not because it is easy. Relatively few people have the ability and the stamina to make it in sales. You undoubtedly do because you are willing to learn new techniques. Most of your colleagues don't even do this.

One of the reasons that there are so few superstars in our profession is because so few people pay the total price for success. Part of that price is asking for the order and not taking the initial no for an answer.

People avoid making decisions for a variety of reasons. They may be afraid, they may need additional information, they may not have the money and are too embarrassed to tell you, or they may have other reasons. Very rarely will they give you the actual reason for their hesitancy. Instead, most people try to "sugar-coat," or hide, the real reasons.

In reality, resistance is usually the result of disagreement or lack of information. Remember that people only hear small portions of what you actually tell them. Often they'll think about a question while you are talking and mull over that question until presented with an opportunity to ask it. That is one of the primary reasons to regularly employ questions like, "How does that sound?" within your presentation. This helps ensure that key client questions or concerns are addressed at the appropriate time. Otherwise, the client might be thinking about his question and not listening to the balance of your presentation. If he is thinking about something else, he is not hearing you.

Any Objection Is Valid
Because the Client Said It

This is an important attitude for you to adopt, because it helps you respond in a more appropriate manner. People are generally afraid of sounding dumb. Many hesitate to express their own opinions. If your response has any harsh tonal qualities, your answer could easily be thought of as a put-down. They'll stop asking and will feel resentful. You will lose the sale.

Our external responses (body language, tonal qualities, etc.) are an excellent reflection of our internal beliefs. If you have a negative or critical attitude, it is too easy to make an unconscious slip. Another way of saying it is, "What you are thinking on the inside is reflected on the outside."

With the correct attitude, however, you realize that the client did not hear or did not understand. It then becomes perfectly reasonable to explain a particular point again. However, there is perhaps an even more important point.

People may also disagree with or have a concern about some aspect of the product or service. The most advantageous attitude for you to have is "Thank you for letting me know about another hot button." The client is telling you what it will take to convince him. If you can satisfy the client's concern, you probably have the sale. If not, then perhaps the product isn't quite as appropriate for the client as you had originally hoped.

How to Handle the Most
Common Objections

There are a few standard objections that salespeople hear over and over again. In most cases you can easily handle these objections by adopting a curious attitude and asking additional questions. Remember, in most cases you will get good, useful information that you can use now or sometime in the future. Always do your best to get the sale, but be gentle. Preserve the potential of the long-term relationship.

"Let Me Think It Over"

"I can appreciate your need to think it over. What exactly do you need to think about?" Or, "In my experience, your needing to think it over is an indication that I didn't fully explain something. Would you be willing to share with me what I should have explained more fully?"

At this point one of two things can happen: (1) the client really does need to think about it, or (2) you discover which "piece of the puzzle" the client is missing.

If part of the client's decision-making strategy (see Chap. 17) is a need for time, then there is nothing that you should do about it. Merely build that into your future conversations by saying something like "I think you should think about this for a couple of days. I'll get back with you then." This way, you have beaten your client to the punch.

You now add, "Is there some information I can get you in the meantime?" If there were any unstated concerns, they'll probably come out now. The client is psychologically "off the hook" about making an immediate decision and probably has her guard down. Hence, you will probably get the information you need to make the sale right then or when you speak to the client next.

"Send Me Some Literature"

"I'd be happy to send you information. So that I only send you the information that you specifically need, please let me know what you want." Again, the client will provide you with information that represents his key motivators. Some people must *see* things before they can make decisions. Others need to *hear* from others. Regardless of clients' visual or auditory orientation, you should take their needs into careful consideration.

"I Have to Talk to My Spouse...Accountant...Attorney..." Etc.

Fair enough. Many people do have a need to discuss major items with an adviser. If this is the case, you would probably be wise to encourage a meeting with the other person. At least you would be able to present the full information in the most favorable light. Remember that the client would not have heard most of what you said and probably forgot most of what he heard. The client is, therefore, not the ideal person to be making the presentation for you.

Many other people use this objection as a way of postponing the decision. By questioning a client about exactly who she needs to talk to and what she needs to talk to that person about, you *may* train your client to make a decision on a more timely basis, which will increase your efficiency in the future sales with this person.

Most of the time you can avoid this situation by asking, early in the conversation, whether another person will be involved. If yes, then you know what to expect. If, however, the answer is no, then you may wish to explore the client's comfort level and work a bit harder at a close.

"The Price Is Too High"

At this point the client has probably already indicated a positive acceptance of your idea. However, there is a question regarding value received versus price paid. Your job is to determine "high in comparison to what?"

You should be able to do an analysis of features and benefits versus costs. It is also helpful to know precisely what your competition is charging.

Very rarely is price the total concern. Many people are very willing to pay a higher price if they feel they are getting superior returns in other areas. Certain cars are purchased because they offer greater status. Price may not be an object if the customer's primary motive is to feel good. Other people may be willing to pay a higher price if they know that the service they receive will be superior.

Finally, some people may say the price is too high just to find out how you react. After all, experience has shown that not everyone is totally honest.

In all cases react by exploring what the prospect meant by the objection and how he or she made that determination. Get specific information and use the techniques of fogging and questioning to get even more information..

Another truism is that people don't mind paying a little bit extra to a salesperson they like, respect, and trust. Use your rapport skills. Be the sales professional that people want to deal with. Think about it, if you had a friend in sales you would probably want to help him out by buying from him and recommending him to others. This is how you want others to think about you.

"I Don't Think This Is for Me"

"Why?" You will probably receive another important piece of information about the client. Take that information and factor it into your subsequent conversation. Of course, you may discover that the client is right, and that the product or service is wrong for them. At that point, be a professional and recommend that he or she do something different. You will have made a friend who will give you referrals and who will come back to you when the time is right.

"I Want to Shop Around"

"Why?" The same logic described in the previous questions applies to this one. When you find out why, you will get the reason behind the excuse. In many situations it is perfectly reasonable to do comparison shopping. Trying to push a person into an immediate sale will only generate resentment.

Use your rapport skills, try to be as helpful as you can, and there is a good probability that the client will return.

P.S. There's no reason that you shouldn't get the prospect's name and phone number so that you can follow up.

"I Just Don't Know"

"What do you need to know that would make a difference for you?" Pay careful attention to the eyes at this point because they will usually indicate whether the client needs to see, hear, or feel something.

In Conclusion

If someone objects, hesitates, or needs additional information, discover what is needed and try to close again. You have the sale to gain. Many sales professionals anticipate trying to close at least three times before they get the sale. The stall or objection merely becomes an indication that the process is working as it should.

20
Getting Referrals

Regardless of what you sell, getting referrals is an excellent source of new business. There are many star performers who obtain over 80 percent of their new business in this manner. Satisfied clients will let their friends and associates know about you, but you must let them know that you both want and accept referrals. It is surprising how many people would be absolutely pleased to give you a recommendation.

This chapter will provide ideas on how to maximize your efforts, including discussions on:

- Maintaining good service
- Asking for referrals
- Effective networking

Maintaining Good Service

A major factor in receiving referrals is providing good service. Many salespeople start to take their clients for granted. Taking the other person for granted doesn't work in personal relationships, and it certainly doesn't work in business relationships. While they were still prospects, the clients were promised the sun, the moon, and the stars if only they became clients. "You will get the best service possible," they were promised. Then they became clients, and the honeymoon was over. The salesperson failed to live up to all the promises, and the clients became some other salesperson's prospects and were wooed away.

As you periodically keep in touch after the initial sale, try to upgrade your value to the customer. You can do this by periodically calling to find out how your product is performing, whether the customer has additional needs, sending him or her product updates or information on new products. All of these things show that you care.

It may seem like time, money, and effort that is better spent somewhere else, but remember that you are developing your referral business. You will be constantly keeping your name in front of the person and occasionally reminding him or her to keep you in mind. You should consider sending birthday and holiday cards to your clients. It won't be too long before you are considered a close associate and perhaps a friend of the family.

There are some super sales stars who very strongly recommend this approach. They attribute much of their success to maintaining good service and keeping their names in front of others.

Asking for Referrals

The best way to get referrals is to ask for them. Start with friends, family members, associates, and anyone else who has an interest in seeing you do well. Make them conscious of your desire to expand your business. The referral ideas presented in Chap. 1 are applicable here. The approach remains virtually identical, "I'm pleased that I was able to assist you and would welcome the opportunity to assist some of your friends or family members. Who in your [choose one] neighborhood/club/church/profession/family might I be able to contact?"

Another method is to send out a nice card or letter that says something like: "From time to time you may meet someone who has a need for our services. I would appreciate it if you would give them my name. It has been a pleasure working with you, and I am looking forward to assisting you in the future. Thank you again for any assistance that you may provide." Make sure that you enclose a few of your business cards for distribution.

Asking for Advice

People love to help others if given the opportunity. If you ask someone for advice, he or she will give it with pleasure. Why not ask some of your clients for advice on how you might get additional customers? They'll probably think of many ways that you haven't considered. They become mentally attuned to search for opportunities for you, and some of them are going to give you great ideas. One idea that almost everyone comes up with is recommending you to any friend or associate they can think of.

One of our students took this recommendation and hit the jackpot. Not only did his client provide a list of names but the client also had pamphlets posted on various bulletin boards throughout the company. Our student received numerous phone calls from company employees and eventually a call from the company president for both a personal and a major corporate purchase.

Effective Networking

Maximize your networking system. For example, did you ever think about inviting a few of your clients and their advisers or friends to a private seminar on the changing needs of your industry? The information may be able to help them in their business.

You can invite clients to special seminars that would be of interest to them and require only that they bring a friend. Your clients get to know each other, and you become a center of influence.

You can do the same thing at a client's home — sort of a Tupperware party. Your client invites a few friends over to his or her house for a private seminar that you will conduct. Because you are there, you are deemed a member of the group of friends and will probably get a few accounts.

Each of your current prospects or clients can be considered the center of their own network of friends. Just join five or six networks. Even if you were only able to convince a small percentage of your clients to hold these parties, you would still make numerous contacts.

If you allow people to assist you, they will love you for it. Being extremely referral-conscious is probably the easiest and most effective way to increase your business. It only works for the sales professional who is doing an excellent job. Perhaps this is one of the many rewards for doing the right thing for others — they return the favor.

It is frequently, although not always, true that the most successful people succeed because they deserve to.

21

Six Questions That Will Generate More Sales

Getting new clients is only half the battle. The other half is getting more money from the clients you already have. This is called account penetration. Many clients have more money and needs than are ever discovered by their sales representative. This is true of virtually every salesperson that we've ever met or even heard about. The best salespeople realize this and are constantly searching for ways to more completely satisfy their clients' needs. They are constantly asking additional penetrating questions and presenting additional ideas. As a result, they uncover needs that the average salesperson never even imagines exist—with a corresponding increase in compensation.

The Odds Are 100 to 1

The odds are 100 to 1 that you'll be amazed with the results of the following experiment. Ask the following questions to about 20 of your best accounts, and you'll undoubtedly be amazed by their answers.

- Can you possibly think of a couple of additional ways that I may be of help to you?
- What could you have used that I failed to offer you?
- Do you have any friends or associates that I may be able to help? (This

could include people in other departments or divisions within the same company. It could even include people at other organizations.)

- How, specifically, may I better serve your needs in the future?
- Are you aware of the full extent of our product line?
- What could my company do to earn more of your business?

Pick the questions that seem best and adapt them to your own style. Then, ask 20 of your accounts. The very best salespeople are constantly asking these or similar questions. We are sure that you'll find the answers both educational and rewarding.

PART 7

Empower Yourself for Sales Success

This section will probably have some of the most important material you ever read. No kidding. It has within it many of the secrets of success and happiness. No, it's not hocus-pocus but rather bottom-line psychological techniques that allow you to direct your energies toward personally worthwhile goals.

"What the mind can conceive, it can achieve," was a statement made by William James, a founder of modern psychology, and it has been proven again and again.

People are constantly programming themselves for either success or failure through mental rehearsals. The brain is like a computer and will accept almost any input it receives. It can receive input and data which empower it, or it can receive information which defeats it. It is totally up to you to choose what information to accept and how to use that information.

Think about it. Do you mentally rehearse certain conversations? How about when you are angry and would like to tell someone off? Do you recall how you feel insulted after an argument and mentally review the incident and all the things you should have said? Virtually everyone has done this. Those I'll-get-you-back scenarios are well known. Equally well known are the fear and anger rehearsals, in which we mentally program ourselves with worry and doubt. The alternative, of course, is to program ourselves with successful thoughts.

Visualization techniques, mental rehearsals, and methods of creating positive mental sets have been around for ages. It is only recently that scientists have discovered the mind-body link and how our thoughts affect us physically. We become what we think. Fortunately, we can choose what we think and how we think (the subject of this part).

In sports, experiments have demonstrated that mental rehearsal is as important as physical rehearsal, or practice. One of the most well known experiments involved proficiency in basketball. A group of students was divided into three smaller subgroups. Subgroup 1 physically practiced basketball every day. Subgroup 2 mentally practiced basketball and did not touch the ball. Subgroup 3 had no practice of any kind.

Some time later the three groups were tested. As expected, subgroup 3 had no improvement. Also as expected, subgroup 1, which had physically practiced throwing the ball on a regular basis, made dramatic improvements. What was fascinating was that the members of subgroup 2, who mentally practiced, did almost as well as those students who physically practiced.

Similar results are found in many other sports. It is now accepted that mental rehearsal has significant effect on performance and is a technique used by many professional sports teams.

An equally interesting concept is mental plus physical rehearsal, to get the best of both worlds. Those athletes who practice physically and mentally substantially outperform their counterparts who may only practice physically.

This section will teach you how you can empower yourself to better performance. The techniques work, but they do require practice. The results will definitely be worth the effort.

22

Visualizing Your Way to Success

This chapter will present some fascinating ways to condition your reactions. You'll learn how to neutralize unwanted feelings and responses. You'll also be introduced to methods which will allow you to program yourself for success. These techniques will work well in combination with those discussed in Chaps. 23 and 24.

Components of Thoughts, Memories, and Experiences

As explained in Chap. 12, everything that we experience comes through the five senses, sight, sound, feeling, taste, and smell. We process information (think and remember) by using mental equivalents or representations of the senses, that is, most people think by using pictures and/or sounds and/or feelings.

How about You?

For instance, now, before you read any further, think about any three things that you did this month. Close your eyes and remember them now. What aspect of the memory did you recall first? Did a scene initially flash into your mind? Or was it a sound or a feeling? Were you aware of the visual, auditory, and feeling components? Or was one aspect not immediately available to your conscious mind? Think about something at the office or at home. Replay it in your mind. Which aspect—sight, sound, feeling, smell, or taste—were you first aware of? Which aspect were you most aware of? Least aware of?

The previous experiment demonstrates four things: (1) thoughts are composed of sensory components called modalities; (2) our minds tend to recall one particular modality first; (3) even though most experiences have all five sensory components, certain components may be initially unavailable to the consciousness; (4) each aspect of memory has sub-components such as color, focus, pitch, rhythm, etc., which are called submodalities. Submodalities will be more thoroughly discussed after the next experiential exercise, in which you'll be taken for a ride, figuratively. Take your time with this next exercise.

Exercise with Submodalities

Pick some enjoyable ride that you have taken (car, rollercoaster, motorcycle, airplane, bicycle, etc.) and mentally pretend that you are watching yourself on a television screen. Be aware of your feelings as you observe yourself going through the experience and the changes in your feelings as you try the various suggestions. (At this point the important idea is whether your feelings change intensity, not whether the changes are more or less pleasurable.)

- Make the television screen the size of a large movie screen. Do your feelings change as the picture becomes bigger?

- What happens if you sit very far from the screen so that it is no larger than a postage stamp?

- Return the picture to the original size and make the picture very bright...then very dark. Was there a change in the intensity of your feelings?

- Try changing the components of sound, making any sounds much louder, then much softer, then shut off the volume entirely. Were there any changes in the feelings attached to this memory?

- What if you make the memory a single snapshot or a moving picture?

Now try reliving the experience as if it is happening to you right at this moment. See it again now, hear it again now, and feel those feelings again. Reexperience it as fully as possible.

What was the difference in the intensity of your feelings between watching yourself on television and reliving the experience? The intensity of experiences tends to increase as we relive (become associated with) a memory. The dissociated state (watching yourself on television) tends to be less intense for most people. The differences in the pictures or sounds (light/dark, near/far, etc.) are the submodalities.

Below you will be asked to step into the past and make a series of submodality changes as you relive a pleasant memory. (Again, the purpose is to verify in your personal experience that certain submodality changes result in a change in feeling intensity.) These simple changes should be made in the midst of the experience (making modifications of what you saw or heard), that is, you are changing the components of memory. Again, for each modification, be aware of the change in feeling intensity that may occur.

Making a Good Memory Even Better

Recall a pleasant experience, perhaps a particularly enjoyable conversation with someone you enjoy being with.

Visual Changes. Be aware of feeling intensity changes as you do each of these.

Make what you are seeing much darker, then much brighter.

Make certain aspects more or less focused.

Try zooming in on part of the scene, then zooming out.

Make the movie much faster, then much slower.

Make any visually oriented variation you choose.

Auditory Changes. Be aware of feeling intensity changes as you do each of these.

Make any sounds much louder, then much softer.

Change the direction that the sounds are coming from: in front, behind, from the left, from the right.

Change the tempo so that the sounds are much faster, then much slower.

Make any variation in the sound that you choose.

Feeling Changes. Be aware of feeling intensity changes as you do each of these.

Make the environment much warmer, then much colder.

Have the entire feeling be located in only one part of your body, then have it spread throughout your body.

Become more aware of any tactile aspects, then less aware.

Make any change in sensation that you choose.

Having gone through this phase of the exercise, you were almost certainly able to change the intensity of the experience as you made some of the suggested changes. It is important to realize that you can change your feelings by changing the way you remember (or anticipate) events. To a very large degree *many of your feelings are subject to your conscious control.*

The final aspect of this exercise is to relive the experience one more time, making a series of changes which enhance the pleasure of the experience. A brief list of some of the submodality changes is provided below. Remember, take this or any other pleasant experience and make the memory much better and more intensely pleasurable. Vary each of the components and, as you vary it, leave it at the point which gives you the best feeling. (Note that some of the variations will result in large intensity changes, while others will provide no conscious effect.) In either case, your very enjoyable job is to increase your own pleasure. Have fun and enjoy yourself.

Visual	Auditory	Kinesthetic
color	volume	temperature
focus	pitch	location
speed	direction	pulse
contrast	rhythm	pressure
brightness	tempo	texture
distance	tone	intensity
clarity	frequency	movement

The submodality listing above represents a few of the more than 50 variations that can be made. Variations of these techniques can allow you to neutralize unpleasant memories and associations. By modifying how you remember something you modify the feelings associated with it. This alone can give you more control over your performance.

A Mental Technique for
Avoiding Bad Feelings

In Chap. 16, "Handling Anger and Hostility—While Getting Sales Information," you were promised a technique which would allow you to
feel more neutral regarding criticism directed toward you. If you have
intense feelings about being insulted or criticized, you need to keep control—unless you like no-win fights. This means having a neutral reaction. We find one way to remain calm is to learn to mentally stand back.
If you have an idea in your head that you react badly to criticism, identify that image. For most people it will be a picture or a voice that says it
is time to feel bad. Try this trick to get rid of that image.

In the three-dimensional material world, if you saw a tiger in the distance it would have less effect on you than if it were right next to you.
In the mind's imagery, the same holds true. If a nasty picture or voice in
your mind is sensed as close it can bother you more than if it is sensed
as far away. Whether voice or picture, imagine moving the unwanted
image away from you so that, as the voice or picture grows distant, it
fades far away and disappears. Repeat this, pushing away the image five
or six times very rapidly. As it fades into the distance each time make
sure you stop and then start the pushing away afresh. Don't pull the
image in and out like a yo-yo, or this technique won't work. Give your
head a shake or do something to break the state between each pushing-
away cycle. You will wind up with a rather neutral reaction.

A dissociated mental state is one where you are so uninvolved and in
control that you feel about as much emotion as you do when having a
cup of coffee. At this point you are able to easily use the verbal techniques for handling difficult situations.

In Closing

Your feelings, positive, neutral, and negative, are a function of how you
choose to remember things. While the techniques you have learned are
just the tip of the iceberg, you have learned enough to enhance the positives and to offset the negatives. That is important, because you can
now take control of your emotions and use them for your benefit.

23
Self-Assessment and Goals

By now, you have an indication of how powerful your mind is when you apply efficient and effective techniques. You can accomplish virtually everything that you want but only when your full energies can be directed toward the effort.

A Case Study in Failure

Sam told the interviewer, "I want to be a top salesman and I'm really willing to work hard to achieve that goal." Sam told the boss the same thing and was eventually hired to sell real estate. After a couple of months it was obvious that Sam was struggling and starting to feel depressed.

When asked for the reasons for his poor performance, Sam indicated that he just couldn't get any prospects. Sam promised to redouble his efforts and, shortly thereafter, quit in disgust. He has followed a similar pattern from one job to the next and will probably continue like this until he learns to get out of his own way.

Little does he know that he has an internal conflict which stops him just short of his goal. Essentially, he sabotages himself.

A Case Study in Success

Samantha was hired at a different agency around the same time as Sam. She also had difficulties, but when her boss tried to help, he asked her a few additional questions that made a huge difference in her life. He first determined if she knew how to do the job. They explored all aspects of the job from how to handle operational problems to what to say to prospective clients. She knew the key things.

Next they explored whether Samantha had the chance to do the job. Were there any things that prevented her from contacting clients? Were her letters going out on time? Was the territory large enough?

Finally, they explored the want-to stage and discovered that Samantha had an unconscious, internal conflict: if she made too many appointments, it would force her to give up her charitable work at the children's hospital. When this was brought to light, they were able to reschedule her time so that she could be both successful and help the children. She became a star.

What about You?

Unless you are 100 percent satisfied with your current level of performance, you may wish to discover which factor or factors might be slowing you down. Below is an evaluation form which helps identify reasons behind performance issues. Read it carefully; many people become very pleasantly surprised when they come to certain realizations.

Self-Diagnostic Performance Evaluation

The *causes* of performance can be divided into three major categories that determine the reasons for such performance. You can use these questions to assess your performance capabilities and/or limitations and as a way of assessing what you may need.

Basically, performance questions can fall into three basic areas: (1) Do you *Want to* achieve your objectives? (2) Do you know *How to* achieve your objectives? (3) Do you have the *Chance to* achieve your objectives?

The following questions represent items that have been observed as frequent factors in performance. Stated another way, the questions elicit whether you have the motive, the means, and the opportunity to succeed.

Do you Want To:

- Do what is required?
- Work for the kinds of incentives and payoffs that the job offers?
- Have more or less independence and power than the job allows?
- Have more or less supervision than offered?

- Achieve the same outcomes and goals as the boss?
- Have more or less social contact than the job allows?
- Hide something that would embarrass you or them?
- Get along with others as required or as necessary?
- Be competitive and assertive as needed?
- Stay in the job for the wrong reasons (e.g., status rather than job interest)?
- Resolve conflicts about the job (such as shyness in an aggressive job: beliefs and self-images that conflict with the job)?

Do you know How To:

- Perform the procedures and techniques necessary to do the job?
- Use strategy for solving the problems that occur on the job?
- Use political or persuasive skills to get cooperation?
- Establish habits for time, stress, deadline, delegation, people and project management, as well as flexible strategies and tactics?
- Use interpersonal and technical skills?
- Elicit cooperation? Motivation? Coordination? Sell ideas?
- *Sound* like you have the skill to camouflage any weak know-how?
- Do the job's technical aspects?

Do you have the Chance To do the job as it is set up, that is, do you have:

- The authority to match the responsibility?
- The right kind of position and title to elicit cooperation from others inside and outside of the company?
- The information, tools, and working conditions you need?
- The right incentives and payoffs to motivate you to work?
- The right kind of supervision to elicit your skills, rapport, and cooperation?
- Impossible deadlines, goals, or conflicting demands of equal priority?
- The fiscal or human or technical resources to do the job?
- Accurate feedback on performance needed to correct performance?

What to Do Next

If you find you do not Want To do the job, then an exploration of needs and motivations is usually in order. The "Defining My Outcome" questionnaire, below, will assist in this process.

If you do not know How To do a job, then the usual solution is additional training. Ask questions. Read books. Have someone provide a demonstration. Practice.

If you do not have the Chance To do the job, then either change the job, change the environment, or go somewhere where the opportunity to succeed exists. If you don't have the opportunity, all of the knowledge and desire is for nothing. If you are not allowed to win, play the game somewhere else or play a different game.

What I Thought I Wanted Isn't What I Really Wanted

You undoubtedly know people who are usually dissatisfied. It seems that they are not getting what they want out of life. Sometimes there are environmental factors which cannot be controlled. However, more often than not, it is their lack of direction that causes the problem. "If you don't know where you're going, any direction is good."

A primary characteristic of the best performers in all professions is a clear understanding of their goals. They know what they want and what it will take to get it. They are able to create a burning desire which keeps them going during the rough periods. It cannot be overemphasized how important it is to your long-term success to clarify your goals.

Defining Your Outcome

Determining your needs and motivations can be very effective in helping you achieve your goals. It is a powerful technique, as the legend of King Midas will illustrate: King Midas loved gold and prayed to the gods that everything he touched should be turned to gold. He was granted his wish and, as is often the situation in life, got more than he bargained for. Everything he touched turned to gold—including his wife, his children, and his food.

The old adage "Be careful of what you ask, for you may get it" applies here. Your outcome or outcomes from this procedure should be very carefully defined because *you will get exactly and precisely what you want.* (Chap. 24 will discuss a procedure for creating new automatic responses. The questions that you answer now will allow that procedure to be very effective.)

Defining My Outcome

Consider each of the following questions carefully. Think about the answer, or perhaps it would help to write it down. Space is provided for this purpose.

- What do I want to do, achieve, be? (How would I like to be different?)

- Is my outcome stated in positives so that there is something specific to move toward rather than simply something I don't want? (For example, "I want to be more enthusiastic" rather than "I don't want to be bored.")

- Is the outcome within my control? (Is it something that I can individually accomplish? You should not put your fate into someone else's hands.)

- How will I look, sound, and feel once I achieve this outcome? (For example, "I'll stand tall with my shoulders back." "My voice will sound confident." "I'll feel good about myself when I'm like this.")
     Look:
     Sound:
     Feel:

- When, where, with whom, and under what circumstances do I want this outcome or behavior?
     When:
     Where:
     With whom:
     Under what circumstances:

- When would I *not* want this outcome? When would it be inappropriate? (There are almost always circumstances or situations when a particular behavior would work to your disadvantage. Think carefully about this.)

- How will I know for sure that I have achieved it? What will be the proof that I have it? (Be sure you have defined your outcome specifically. Very often people will say "I want *x*," but if you haven't defined what that means, how are you going to know when you have it?)

- How will this outcome affect other areas of my life?
  Social:
  Mental:
  Emotional:
  Family:
  Professional:
- Will this outcome help me achieve other things in my life? How?
- Is this outcome really worth pursuing? How do I know?

What You Can Expect

These questions ensure that you have taken many factors into consideration. They help ensure that conflicting goals (conscious or unconscious) are resolved. They help you get going in the right direction.

If you have answered these questions carefully, you will find yourself going forward with a power that most people only imagine. You can further enhance your goal by using the techniques presented in Chap. 22 to make the goal even more compelling.

Write Your Goals Down

Once you determine what you want, write it down. In 1950, the Ivy League colleges began a study of that year's graduating classes. In answer to the question whether they had established goals for their lives, 87 percent of the graduates said they had not. Ten percent said they had established mental goals, but had not written them down, and only 3 percent said they had developed written goals for their lives.

The schools followed the progress of their graduates for 25 years. In 1975, they found that the 87 percent who had not established goals had performed in an average manner during the intervening years. After attending the most expensive schools in the country, these people had achieved mediocrity. The 10 percent who had established mental goals but had not written them down had outperformed the 87 percent of their classmates without goals. The 3 percent who had developed written goals had outperformed the other 97 percent of their classmates.

By having written goals you have established a benchmark for your performance. It serves as a reminder of where you want to be so that you remain more directed.

In Summary

You have a procedure for assessing your performance and a method to fully clarify your goals. They both allow you the opportunity to fine-tune your efforts so that you maximize your probability of success.

The next chapter will introduce a method to mentally condition yourself to perform in an optimal manner. It helps you to achieve the goals that were determined here.

24
Determining Future Responses

"If Only I'd..."

People often wish that they had acted differently or more appropriately after the fact. "I should have done it this way," or "I wish I hadn't done that," or "Next time that happens I'll..." are common statements. Others wish that they could more precisely match another person's performance. It usually goes no further than a statement of desire or intention. Now, using this technique, rather than sit back and hope, you can ensure that your future actions are the ones which would best serve or further your interests.

The Behavior Generator

The Behavior Generator is a technique which allows you to predetermine how you will act or react in a situation so that your automatic responses will be the ones that are most appropriate and beneficial. This chapter's how-to orientation provides the equivalent of a recipe book for personal change. The suggested exercises ensure hands-on experience. The net result is that you gain more control over your personal performance and tap into more of the vast potentials inherent within you.

Overview

The first step is a series of questions which should be carefully answered. The answers to these questions will be vital in establishing the times and places when the new responses will occur. The second step provides a method where you mentally try out the new behaviors in a riskless environment — the mind. You imagine how you would look and sound performing a certain new behavior or acting in a different way. Once you find that the new behavior is the one you want, you then ensure that it occurs at the appropriate time in the future. For example, we might wish to mentally rehearse how we would react with a certain person, or rehearse a performance.

The pages that follow provide a specific procedure that can be employed by anyone. *It is important to follow the directions precisely* to receive full benefit from the procedure.

The Behavior Generator is divided into three parts:

- Determine how you would like to act in a given situation.
- Modify the new behavior until you are satisfied.
- Establish the future response.

Because this procedure creates a response that will automatically occur in the future, it is important to think about the potential results of your actions. Once you determine which new behavior you want, it becomes a new behavioral option which can be used whenever appropriate and modified based upon changing circumstances.

Specific Procedures

Please read the following thoroughly first so that you are familiar with the terminology and the procedures and will be able to utilize the process effectively.

1. Determine what behavior you would like to have and ask yourself the series of questions from Chap. 23 (repeated here in summary form):
   a. What, exactly, do I want to be able to do, or how do I want to act in a particular situation? (It is vital that you have a goal that you want to achieve and that this goal be stated in a positive manner. "I want to be...," rather than something you do not want. Words like *not, don't,* and *won't* should be avoided. Chapter 14 provides a more complete explanation.)
   b. How would this new response benefit me? When would it be disadvantageous? When would it be appropriate? With whom and under what circumstances would I like to have it?
   c. Is it appropriate for me? Is there any benefit to remaining the way I am?

d. When would it be inappropriate? When would I not want this behavior?

These questions are a *very important* part of the procedure. Be sure of what you want, because this procedure will give it to you. You should be absolutely certain that what you want is totally appropriate for you. For example, a man wanted to be assertive with his boss. He took a course on how to be assertive and learned some worthwhile skills. However, he also became assertive with his wife, which was harmful to his marriage. He inadvertently overdid it. This is why you should pay particular attention to specifically where and with whom you want a new behavior. This self-questioning process also fine-tunes the desired behavior. It allows you to get precise results at the needed time, rather than results which may be only adequate or ones that occur at the wrong time or place.

2. Having decided exactly what you want, you now determine whether you know what to do or how to act in the situation. If you know exactly how you would like to act, then go to step 3. If you're not too sure exactly how you would like to act, you might wish to choose a model, someone to emulate. If so, go to step 2a.

   a. Choose a person that you would like to emulate, that is, think about someone who already does in an elegant way whatever you are trying to learn. You can emulate someone you know or know of. Many people will choose a TV or movie personality. The person you choose should elegantly represent the way you would like to act.

   b. Create a mental movie and watch and listen to that person on a mental screen performing the behavior. At this point you are that person's "understudy." Carefully memorize how that person acts and/or reacts to the situation.

   c. Decide whether or not you would like to act in this manner. If yes, then go to step 3. If not, redirect the scene or decide upon another model and recycle to step 2a. (This recycling procedure is part of the checks and balances built into the procedure and further ensures that the process will be effective.)

3. Create a mental screen on which you may watch and listen to yourself go through a series of experimental behaviors. It is important that you be able to watch yourself role-playing in this mental movie.

4. While observing yourself on this screen, observe and listen to the movie carefully. Do you like your actions? Feel free to modify your actions, reactions, responses etc. Be the movie director. Experiment. Enjoy the process.

a. In addition to modifying your own actions, posture, statements, modify the movie "effects," that is, modify the visual and auditory aspects of the imagined experience until you are completely satisfied. Some of the visual effects that you might change are the focus, brightness, darkness, distance of the screen from you or the distance of the characters from each other, intensity of colors, contrast of shadings, perspective, etc. Some of the auditory effects that you might modify are tone, pitch, volume, rhythm, etc., of the characters. Change any of the components that would make your movie script look or sound better. Make note of which changes cause a positive or negative reaction within you. Keep the effects that you like.

b. If you are less than totally satisfied or slightly uncomfortable watching and listening to your image, then change the script by recycling to step 4, adding additional resources, modifying your physiology, and making additional submodality changes, *or* you might decide that you would like to see how someone else might do it by recycling to step 2 and observing a different role model.

5. When totally satisfied with the imaginary TV or movie script, mentally step into the picture so that you momentarily are "living" the movie. (The purpose is to determine whether the new behavior actually "feels good," whether you really like the new behavior. You'll get a positive or negative feeling at this point.)

a. If *positive*, then you have a potential new behavior and can go to step 6.

b. If *negative*, then step out of the picture, i.e., watch yourself on the screen again, and recycle to step 4 and make additional modifications. At this point, you might wish to concentrate on the "effects" and additional resources.

6. Having found one or more alternative behaviors, it is important to "future-pace" yourself. Imagine a time in the future when you will be in that situation or a similar situation. This is sort of a mental rehearsal in which you condition yourself to employ the new response or behavior at the time you want it.

a. Imagine yourself on the mental screen in that future situation. If it still feels good, go to step 6b. If something doesn't look or sound right, return to step 4.

b. Now, imagine what it would look, sound, and feel like if you were "living" it now—seeing through your own eyes, hearing through your own ears, and being aware of your feelings. If you like your new responses, especially the feelings, continue to the next step. If not, it is important to return to step 4.

c. If you are fully satisfied with step 6b, mentally rehearse your new behavior for at least two additional future situations, that is, repeat steps 6a and 6b for additional times or situations when you want the new behavior in the future. This ensures automatic implementation of the new actions at the appropriate time.

Congratulations! You have completed the process and have installed one or more additional behavioral responses. This process can be continued with additional refinements as your needs change. *Because we cannot control other people and their actions and reactions, it is wise to work on different scenarios so that you have a variety of responses.* This technique can be applied to many areas of your life. It works if you follow the procedures exactly. If you later decide to make modifications or enhancements, merely repeat the process.

The Behavior Generator can be utilized for virtually any situation in which you would like to perform more elegantly and comfortably. It can be combined with even more powerful techniques to give yourself a state of excellence. A thorough reading of the previous material will allow you to easily follow this summarized procedure:

Summary

1. Decide what you want.
2. Do you wish to emulate someone? If no, go to step 3. If yes, (a) choose the person, (b) study that person, and (c) decide if you like what he or she does. Then either go to step 3 or choose someone else to emulate.
3. Observe yourself on a mental screen.
4. Change the script and the "effects" until you are satisfied or choose another model and recycle to 2a.
5. Momentarily "live" in the movie. Check your feelings. Continue or recycle to step 4.
6. Imagine three future situations by first observing yourself and then "living" them. If you are satisfied, you have completed the procedure. If not, recycle to step 4 and continue until satisfied.

This technique can be applied to many areas of your life. It works if you follow the procedure exactly. You may want to make modifications or enhancements. If so, just follow the procedure again.

It is important to note that you now have conscious control over some of your reactions—perhaps for the first time. You can mentally program personal excellence. Enjoy the process.

Epilogue

You have come a long way. You've learned and done a lot. Whether you are fully satisfied with the past is not as important as the following question: "Where do you want to go from here?" You are the movie producer and director of your future. You also write the majority of the script. What type of movie do you want? A drama?...A comedy?...An adventure story?...Something different?

How about the ending to the story? Will it be a happy ending? I certainly hope so. In reality you are the hero of your own story and can take significant control over how your life story progresses from this point onward.

You have the ability to do virtually anything you want as long as you work for it. This type of work can be fun and highly rewarding because you can choose success. That's right — success is a choice. You can choose to create a series of personal and professional goals that are meaningful to you as an individual relative to your family, friends, and career. If you write them down and then progressively work toward their realization, you can give yourself numerous pats on the back along the way.

Here is a very important point. You can be doing something (even resting may count) toward one of your goals regularly so that you are in the process of "successing." Successing is an ongoing process that allows you to feel good, proud, and happy regularly. A series of daily successes allows the intermediate and longer-term goals to be accomplished. However, you'll enjoy yourself along the way.

As you think about your future, remember to ask yourself the various questions represented by Want To, How To, Chance To and Real — Win — Worth and the additional questions to Defining Your Outcome. This will ensure that you apply your time and energies in a very effective manner. It helps avoid the situation that many others fall into of being "scattered," "stuck," "demotivated," or whatever name they give to doing nothing and going nowhere.

You must rely on yourself and start now. Once you commit yourself to your happy ending and actually begin, things really start to happen. As Goethe said:

> *Until one is committed, there is hesitancy, the chance to draw back, always ineffectiveness. Concerning all acts of initiative (and creation), there is one elementary truth—the ignorance of which kills countless ideas and splendid plans: that the moment one definitely commits oneself, then Providence moves, too.*
>
> *All sorts of things occur to help one that would never otherwise have occurred. A whole stream of events issues from the decision, raising in one's favor all manner of unforeseen incidents and meetings and material assistance, which no man could have dreamed would have come his way. Whatever you can do, or dream you can, begin it. Boldness has genius, power and magic in it. Begin it now.*

Two sayings apply here: "The journey of a thousand miles begins with the first step," and "How do you eat an elephant? One bite at a time." You've already taken many of the first steps. You've already traveled a good distance. You already have skills which will get you to where you are going. But do you want to travel down the road using low gear or high gear? Both will get you where you want to be, yet high gear is much more efficient when you really wish to go far.

High gear has many aspects. The one part already mentioned deals with your personal motivation and goals and how you deal with yourself. The other part is concerned with dealing with other people in a way that maximizes your successes.

The systematic approach to sales excellence you have just learned emphasizes the need to deal with the individual, rather than the generic, client. You have learned to be flexible in your approach.

It is vital to your professional development to respond to what is happening instead of to what should be happening. Communication is like a dance—while you wish to lead your partner, you must also respond to your partner. It is the same with sales, management, parenting, and family relationships. You lead a person to a conclusion by helping, not dragging, him or her along. You help by employing the other person's own ideas, beliefs, and needs.

If you have a fixed opinion about other people's behavior, you will miss a great deal of useful information. The odds that your guesses are going to be correct are much less than 50-50. That is also known as chance. You can't afford to run your career on chance. You need to run your career on tools that are useful in any situation involving persuasion.

*Truly effective sales presentations are based upon the way a person ac-
tually thinks, by using your observations of the client's key buying motivations, thought sequence, and personal characteristics to significantly increase the probability of closing the sale. This means using both his or her
conscious and unconscious thought processes. You've learned to make
your presentations truly individualized and highly effective. Your success
ratios will be greatly increased as you regularly apply your knowledge.*

*You have tools to understand people on a multitude of levels. You can
learn what motivates them, how they actually think, and what to say to
persuade them. However, these tools must be used. These skills need to be
honed.*

*The effective acquisition of any skill initially requires conscious atten-
tion. Could you learn to ride a bicycle or drive a car by merely reading a
book? The intellectual knowledge might be there, but could you do it easily, naturally, and elegantly the first time you tried it? Of course not. It
would require practice, with the understanding that each practice session
adds to and refines the skill until you can do it automatically.*

*The skills presented in this book pose a similar challenge. By reading,
you've gotten an intellectual understanding of the various skills; you
know when they can and should be used and generally how to use them.
But, like learning to operate a bicycle or a car, you need to be able to
actually do it. Reading is not enough. So use the techniques and work
them into your style.*

*If you would like to make more money, then make your decision and go
for it. There are numerous things that you can do to ensure this. Foremost
is your ability to take responsibility for the things you can control. You
can't control the environment. You can't control whether your client will
have money available or will like your idea. But you can control your own
personal performance. You can decide to make x number of calls each
day. You can decide to qualify x number of prospects each day. And you
can decide to make x number of presentations each day. When you make
this decision to do no less than a certain x amount of work each day, you
guarantee your ultimate success.*

*That's enough for now. It's time to say good-bye. I'm sure you can make
it big in this business if you choose to make it big. But there is the price of
work to be paid. The reward is the things and enjoyment that money can
bring to you and your family. I wish you health, happiness, and prosperity
in all your endeavors.*

Index

About the Authors

STEVEN DROZDECK is president of Training Groups, Inc., which specializes in performance-oriented sales, management, and quality control training. He has trained over 20,000 people in sales and management and is coauthor with Karl Gretz of *Consultative Selling for the Financial Professional, The Effective Manager*, and *Empowering Creative People*.

JOSEPH YEAGER serves as a management consultant to many *Fortune* 100 companies and is a practicing psychologist. He is the author of *Thinking about Thinking with NLP* and numerous articles on management, consulting, and behavioral science. He is president of the consulting firm, Linguis-Techs.

LINDA SOMMER is an organizational consultant to *Fortune* 100 companies in the area of human resources. She is a popular speaker on communication and develops behavior change programs for management development and individual and group coaching. She is president of CommTech Group Inc., a consulting firm.

FOR FURTHER INFORMATION

The authors can be contacted through:

Training Groups, Inc.
P.O. Box 996
Newtown, PA 18940
(215)968-9292
(215)860-0911

Training in all aspects of effective communication is offered to individuals and corporations. Programs in sales, management, and customer service are tailored to meet specific corporate needs.

Please call or write for a list of our programs, products, and services. We would be pleased to put you on our mailing list.

Additionally, we would appreciate your feedback on this book and hope that we can be of future service to you.